NOT JUST ANOTHER QUILT

NOT
JUST
ANOTHER
QUILT

Sarah Doolan Gobes
Mickey Lawler
Sheila Meyer
Judy Robbins

VNR VAN NOSTRAND REINHOLD COMPANY
NEW YORK CINCINNATI TORONTO LONDON MELBOURNE

Copyright © 1982 by Van Nostrand Reinhold Company Inc.
Library of Congress Catalog Card Number 82-2816
ISBN 0-442-22054-5

Printed in the United States of America
Design by Sharen DuGoff

Published by Van Nostrand Reinhold Company Inc.
135 West 50th Street, New York, NY 10020

Van Nostrand Reinhold Publishing
1410 Birchmount Road
Scarborough, Ontario M1P 2E7, Canada

Van Nostrand Reinhold Australia Pty. Ltd.
17 Queen Street
Mitcham, Victoria 3132, Australia

Van Nostrand Reinhold Company Limited
Molly Millars Lane
Wokingham, Berkshire, England

16 15 14 13 12 11 10 9 8 7 6 5 4 3 2 1

Library of Congress Cataloging in Publication Data
Main entry under title:

Not just another quilt.

   Includes index.
   1. Quilting. I. Gobes, Sarah Doolan.
TT835.N67   746.9′7041   82-2816
ISBN 0-442-22054-5   AACR2

DEDICATION

Our special thanks to
Talbott and Todd;
Muffy, Terry, and Katie;
Tobie, Stephanie, and Jessica;
Jeffrey, Neil, and Timothy;
and particularly Jim, Dan, Roger, and Bruce
for love, patience, and support.

I want to say something to all of you
who have become a part
of the fabric of my life.

The color and texture
which you have brought into my being
have become a song
and I want to sing it forever.

There is an energy in us
which makes things happen
when the paths of other persons
touch ours
and we have to be there
and let it happen.

When the time
of our particular sunset comes
our thing, our accomplishment
won't really matter a great deal.

But the clarity and care
with which we have loved others
will speak with vitality
of the great gift of life
we have been for each other.

Contents

NOT JUST ANOTHER QUILT

Introduction

The popularity of quilting is evident from the books, booklets, and magazine articles we see devoted to it. Those beautiful, traditional quilt patterns we've all grown to know and love are readily available in any number of sources. One need only look. But what about those of us who like the process of quiltmaking (or who would like to try it for the first time), but prefer a more modern look to our hand-crafted projects? There are dozens upon dozens of traditional quilt patterns around, but where would the person who prefers contemporary quilt patterns look?

Not Just Another Quilt is a pattern and project book of new quilt designs— some flamboyantly contemporary and some contemporary but visibly linked to tradition. All of the designs are original and all of the projects have been made by the authors using readily available materials. The designs are versatile, and the more inventive reader is encouraged to interpret freely. Our primary concern is to communicate our projects simply and clearly.

Quiltmaking, like many revitalized American crafts, is proceeding in an innovative direction. What began as simple reproductions of antique quilts is now contemplated as an art form, and more and more people are seeking to personalize quilts as an expression of contemporary life. However, unless the quiltmaker also has training in art, the choices of quilt designs have, so far, been very limited.

We, as contemporary quiltmakers, are always pleasantly aware of the solid tradition that is the basis for our craft. This tradition influences us in subtle ways because of the many similarities that exist between the work we are doing and that of the earliest quilters.

Each of the patterns we think of as traditional now was original and modern in its own day. Even when economic hardship existed and new fabric was unavailable, there is evidence that the early quilter wanted to create orderliness and balance in her work. She pioneered new designs without the benefit of magazines, quilt books, and graph paper. Her primary resource was her own ingenuity. Lacking the sophisticated tools we

11

have today, the early quilters drew heavily on their innate aesthetic senses to devise the large body of patterns that became so popular. They were copied rather religiously until the late 1960s. It was not until then that a reawakened interest in the art of quilting stimulated some contemporary quiltmakers to break from tradition and go off in new directions, much in the same way that pioneer women did when they became tired of patching squares.

It seems to us that there have always been people who want, perhaps need, to create something original. This is true not only of quilters, but of all people who are involved in any of the creative arts. These people are innovators and their creativity is stifled by repetition of those tried and true traditional patterns. Some women who tired of patching squares decided to split squares into triangles, thus opening up many more design possibilities. And some, we must assume, found new ways to express themselves with fabric by piecing diamonds, hexagons, and other geometric shapes.

At the other end of the creative spectrum are the many people who love the traditional designs and delight in making a *Log Cabin* or *Ohio Star*. They derive their satisfaction from the quilt*making process*, and the beauty of their results, and not from innovative design. We owe these women a debt of gratitude, for without them and the beautiful quilts that they produce, we would not have so many exquisite examples of traditional design today. Often these quilts have given us the inspiration for innovative designs.

It is our hope that this book will appeal to quilters who can execute a traditional pattern well and who have the desire to break out of the mold and create something that is uniquely theirs.

1

The Craft of Quiltmaking

The visual impact of any quilt design, whether traditional or contemporary, is inextricably bound to the craftsmanship of its maker. A basic knowledge of quiltmaking materials and procedures is essential, not to satisfy some critical eye (for there will always be those who confuse the arts with competitive sports), but, rather, to show the colors and design in the most aesthetically pleasing way possible.

In order to arrive at the finished quilt, the quiltmaker must first piece the top, then fasten it to the batting and the back of the quilt. This is, of course, an oversimplification of the quiltmaking process, and these steps may be accomplished in a wide variety of different ways. However, throughout our years of teaching and quiltmaking, we have arrived at methods that work well for us. It is our hope that the procedures and suggestions in this chapter will aid in your own enjoyment of the fascinating art of quiltmaking. Be sure to refer to the Glossary in the back of the book if some of the terms are unfamiliar to you.

FABRICS AND FIBERS

Cotton broadcloth is the most widely recommended fabric for quiltmaking, but, until recently, finding the right 100% cotton was a major chore. All that was available was a small selection of wrinkly 36-inch-wide cloth. Today, however, with new quilt shops opening every week, fabric manufacturers and distributors have awakened to the demands of a vast new market and have provided a wonderful selection of printed and solid 100% cotton.

100% cotton broadcloth is the easiest and most reliable fabric to use in quiltmaking because it can be cut accurately, remains stable when sewn, and presses well. It can be hand quilted easily, yet is still sturdy enough to withstand years of use. Most cotton broadcloth is now 45 inches wide and crease-resistant. Some even comes from the washer and dryer totally wrinkle free. Fine imported cottons also handle beautifully with little wrinkling.

Although 100% cotton is essential for piecing diamonds or long sharp points, such as those in **Easter, Medicine Man,** and **Amethystine** (see pages 71, 78, and 127), most of us will buy a blend if "it's just the right shade of blue" or "the perfect sea-green print." For many pieced quilts a blend is fine. If your design is easy to piece and contains mostly straight edges, a polyester/cotton broadcloth should be suitable. It's wise to remember, though, that a blend is generally softer than 100% cotton, it slides more when cut and sewn, and it may pill after the quilt has been used for some time. It's a good idea to make sure the blend contains at least 35% cotton. Avoid a rayon blend at all costs. The qualities that make rayon lovely for softly draped clothing will turn a quilt into a mass of tiny ripples.

The experienced quilter can usually tell by feeling a fabric whether it will be easy to piece, as well as to quilt, but even the "hand" or feel of the fabric can be deceiving. Many fabrics contain sizing, which will come out with the first wash, leaving the cloth softer than you had anticipated. In some cases this may be to your advantage. A fabric that at first seemed too stiff will be more manageable and easier to quilt. However, an apparently workable fabric may become too limp once the sizing is washed out. When you are choosing a fabric in a store, it is almost impossible to tell how much sizing the fabric may contain. If you have any doubts about your choice, purchase just the minimum amount. Take it home, wash it, then cut and sew a trial block or sample section of the quilt. You will know without investing too much time or money whether this fabric will work for your purposes. If a fabric that you absolutely can't live without should become too soft, spray starch or spray sizing will often add just enough body to enable you to cut and sew it more accurately.

Because it is easy to quilt through, we often prefer a soft cotton blend for the quilt backing. Bedsheets are generally too stiff and densely woven for hand quilting.

Although the fiber content is a prime consideration in any pieced quilt, colors and prints are the irresistible attractions for quiltmakers. Dazzling contrasts or subtle interweavings of shading excite our imaginations so much that many quilts have been designed around a favorite piece of fabric. One fabric by itself, however, is not enough. So we gather in other fabrics to complement both the primary fabric and the quilt design. This is the crucial step. The wrong choice can mask the beauty and distinction, but the right choice creates harmony and vitality.

If you like an old-fashioned or antique look, a grouping of muted prints will achieve that effect. On the other hand, using solid colors exclusively will tend to make even the most traditional design look contemporary. Whichever effect you desire, it's important to choose the fabrics carefully.

A print should be well stamped and its figures distinct. A poor print has a muddy look because the colors run together, whereas an artistically fine print is clear and sharp, and each color is chosen to complement the whole. It stands to reason that good prints are generally more expensive because the manufacturers spend more money on their printing and fabric designers. The colors in a well-designed print tell us which colors will coordinate with that print. For example, if there is a small blue leaf in a basically brown calico, that same blue will work well as a secondary solid or print. If a more complex print contains five or six different colors, all of these colors will work harmoniously together in one quilt.

Since most of us were brought up never to wear a flowered shirt with striped slacks, the use of many prints in one quilt may require some courage. The experienced quiltmaker is often more comfortable with this effect than the novice. It may help to realize that many prints act very much like solids when they have been incorporated into the whole quilt. For instance, small monochromatic calicos or pin-dots can be used as solid colors and will give the effect of textures rather than prints. They are almost always a safe choice with any larger print. A print also diffuses color. An all-red print, for instance, is never as red as a solid red! So a print can be used to achieve shading where the right solid shade is not available.

The use of solid colors offers a distinctly different challenge. Because there is no interruption in the surface design, colors are often more intense than we might first expect, and gradations of shading are sometimes hard to achieve. In Chapter 3 you will find specific suggestions for determining your choice of colors and fabrics. "Fabricgraphing," for example, is one of the best methods to help you decide whether solids will produce the effect you intend in your quilt design.

Once your selection is made, be sure to preshrink your fabrics by washing and pressing them in preparation for marking and cutting the pieces.

BATTINGS

Batting is the layer in the middle of a quilt that gives dimension and loft and, in the case of a bed quilt, warmth. Unless quilting lines are spaced no more than 1 inch apart, cotton batts often create problems by separating and bunching. Polyester batting, on the other hand, allows an area of 4 to 5 inches to be left unquilted. This advantage alone has given us greater freedom in our choice of quilting designs. Polyester batting is the overwhelming preference of today's quiltmaker.

Polyester batting is manufactured by several companies, and there is a distinct difference in quality and texture from one manufacturer to the next. Batts come in different bed sizes, can be "bonded" (that is, glazed to hold the batt together) or unbonded, and are available in various thicknesses. Since most experienced quiltmakers have already developed a preference for one type of batt or another, we'll make just a few basic recommendations. If you are a newcomer, you will surely want to try various brands to discover your own choices.

First, make sure the batting you choose is of uniform thickness throughout and that it has no thin spots. Second, a batting with coarse fibers prevents *bearding* (drifting of the polyester filaments through the outer fabric of the quilt) and is generally more stable and easier to handle than one with fluffy or silky fibers. Third, a flat, compact batt will allow you to take smaller, closer stitches than a thick batt or one with greater loft. Your choice of thickness will depend on the quilting effect you wish for a particular piece. If a quilt requires an intricate quilting design, it would be wise to choose a flat batt. However, if you simply intend to outline-quilt large shapes, you have the option of almost any thickness you wish.

As far as washability is concerned, theoretically, all polyester batts are machine washable and dryable once they are inside the finished quilt. However, some loose or airy unbonded batts tend to flatten and sometimes even disintegrate after repeated washings. Bonded and compact batts, on the other hand, wash and dry very nicely. Look for a batt with coarse fibers to keep its loft well after repeated washing and drying.

TOOLS AND EQUIPMENT

Appropriate, well-made tools can mean the difference between an enjoyable creative experience and a frustrating battle. Even beautiful fabric can be shredded by dull scissors or chewed up by a bad sewing machine. Consider this: a good pair of scissors and fine sewing machine are constructed to last a lifetime. (Can the same be said for an expensive lawn mower or snowblower that is used only half the year?) Your time and talent are worth the best, so make a point of purchasing the finest quality tools.

SEWING MACHINE

A sewing machine is obviously the largest investment you will make. It needn't have a complex assortment of embroidery cams, ruffling attachments, or eyelet makers. Quiltmaking generally requires little more than a good forward and reverse straight stitch, even tension, and a strong motor to sew steadily through multiple layers of fabric. If you already own a good machine, occasionally check the presser foot and throat plate for nicks and scratches. Sewing over pins, as we quiltmakers often do, can damage the smooth metal on the underside of the presser foot and the top of the throat plate. Replace both after a few years so that the rough metal doesn't pull or pill your fabric. And don't forget the sewing machine needles. The needle that came with your machine wasn't meant to last a lifetime and should probably be dead and buried by now. Take a look at it. Perhaps you might make it a practice to insert a new needle each time you begin a new quilt. Although ballpoint needles are great for knits, they should not be used on woven fabrics. Size 14 regular point needles are suitable for most cottons.

SMALL ACCESSORIES

Just as important as a reliable sewing machine is a good pair of scissors. Seven- or eight-inch steel dressmakers' shears that will cut four layers of fabric the entire length of the blade are ideal. Make sure that they can be sharpened when necessary (there are some scissors on the market that cannot be sharpened), and keep them very sharp. Use them only to cut fabric. Cutting other materials (paper, hair, etc.) will render them useless for fabric. A clean, straight cut is most important to ensure accurate piecing, and only very sharp scissors allow you to cut multiple layers with ease.

A thimble that fits comfortably on the middle finger of your sewing hand is also essential. There are various sizes available in metal thimbles, or, for those who find metal thimbles uncomfortable, a leather thimble might be a good alternative. Whichever you choose, a thimble is imperative. In a very short time, pushing stitches through multiple layers with your bare finger will be agonizing. To become accustomed to a thimble, perhaps you might try wearing it around the house when you are not sewing. You will get used to the feel of the thimble without the annoyance of trying to sew at the same time. Before long you may hardly be aware of it. It's worth a try!

Needles and pins are often overlooked when we consider important quiltmaking tools. Could it be that they are so inexpensive by comparison that we just assume any old needle or pin will do? Grandma's quilts may be cherished heirlooms, but she certainly wouldn't want us to revere her bent needles and pins. A new box of pins might be a real treat. The long, thin ones with colored heads are excellent. Avoid ballpoint pins if possible because they are difficult to push through woven cottons. Hand-quilting needles are labeled *betweens* or *quilting needles*, and they range in size from 10 (very short and extremely fine) down to 5 (longer and thicker). It's advisable to purchase a variety package at first to find out which size works best for you.

FRAMES AND HOOPS

Stretching your quilt on a frame or hoop will prevent bunching and shifting while you quilt. Although a large frame, which accommodates the whole quilt at one time, was used for centuries, today's quiltmakers seem to prefer a wooden hoop. Round or oval quilting hoops resemble oversized embroidery hoops, are usually 14 to 24 inches in diameter, and may come with a stand. Your choice is simply a matter of personal preference. Although the large wooden frame is suitable for group quilting, there are several advantages to using the hoop. It takes up very little room, is light-weight and portable, and a quilt may be removed and replaced at any time during its progress. A quilt placed in a large frame, on the other hand, must remain in the frame until it is completed. Since both frame and hoop will accommodate crib-size to king-size quilts, and, since there is no difference in the quality of the results, it's easy to see why the less expensive quilting hoop is gaining popularity.

PATTERN DRAFTING

While many of you may have your own favorite methods of drafting patterns, we would like to recommend two that we feel provide accurate results and use readily available materials.

POSTERBOARD METHOD

Posterboard comes in large white or colored sheets. It is always obtainable in art-supply stores and frequently in variety and drugstores. Because of its large size, you are able to draft one or many quilt blocks—sometimes an entire wall hanging—on one piece. It is inexpensive and durable. We suggest drafting patterns on this, rather than on shirt cardboard, or on any other softer board.

The block should be very carefully drafted to scale on the posterboard to ensure accuracy. Label pieces of posterboard to correspond to letters on patterns, indicating "r" on the reverse side where applicable. If you find drafting too difficult, the patterns given in the project chapters may also be copied on tracing paper, cut out, and glued to the posterboard. Or you may want to use carbon paper to transfer the patterns directly from the book to the posterboard. Once you have completed this step you know that you have a supply of templates that fit together as accurately as your fabric block will. You should cut apart only as many *different* shapes as you need. For example: if there are four identical triangles in the block, you need cut only one template, saving the others for later use in the event the first one becomes worn. And while the posterboard is partially intact, it serves as a sewing guide because you can easily see how the templates fit together. This method is ideal for hand sewing. By cutting ¼ inch outside the pencil line to allow for seams, your piece is ready for hand sewing.

GRAPH PAPER METHOD

Graph paper is a valuable tool if you want to add seam allowances to your templates to enable you to cut or machine sew multiple thicknesses of fabric. A pad of graph paper that is ruled four squares to the inch will allow you to cut your templates exactly ¼ inch larger on all sides. Trace the template on graph paper. Draw lines on the grid ¼ inch larger all around. Cut this out, glue it to the posterboard, then cut out again. You now have an accurate template ready to be traced on your fabric for machine sewing.

Sheets of clear plastic that are ruled like graph paper are also on the market. They can be used to trace patterns directly from the book, thus eliminating the use of glue. The patterns are traced and then cut ¼ inch larger around the shape, which provides you with a permanent template. This method may not be feasible for large templates (because the plastic sheets come in small sizes), but it is handy for making small templates.

TRACING AND CUTTING

In our project chapters we indicate grain lines with arrows on our pattern pieces in the same way a commercial pattern does. It is important to follow these instructions when you are tracing and cutting your pattern pieces. The arrows will enable you to place the templates on your fabric in such a way as to minimize the number of bias sides. (For example, a right angle triangle placed with the base side on the straight grain of the fabric will have the perpendicular side on the crossgrain, so there remains only one side on the bias.) Bias can be used to advantage in certain sewing projects, but quiltmaking is not one of them.

Remove the selvage edges of your fabric, and then trace your templates on the wrong side of your fabric. If the fabric appears to have no right or wrong side, determine which will be the wrong side and be consistent throughout. On light fabrics trace your templates with a pencil or watersoluble pen; use a white or pastel dressmakers' pencil for tracing on dark fabrics. Be sure to allow room for seam allowances between each template.

If you have adapted your templates to include seam allowances, you may allow their edges to touch in order to minimize fabric waste. It is also possible to cut multiple thicknesses of fabric if you have chosen this method. With some strategic pinning and sharp scissors you can cut up to eight layers of fabric; four, however, is probably a safer number.

SEWING

Hand- or machine-sewing methods may be used to piece the designs in this book. In some cases the two methods may be combined in one piece. Most sewers have a definite preference. The confirmed machine sewer is willing to overlook slight inaccuracies in order to complete the project quickly, while the hand sewer accepts the slower pace in exchange for precision piecing.

HAND SEWING

Hand sewing will enable you to piece your quilt or wall hanging with the greatest amount of accuracy, if not speed; but many people find hand sewing so relaxing and the results so neat and attractive that speed is not a consideration.

For hand sewing, the line that you traced on the fabric is your sewing line. Begin by matching your penciled sewing line to the corresponding line on the piece to which it will be attached. Pin these two pieces together first by matching the corners or joints. Then pin every inch or so to secure the pieces for sewing and to ease in any fullness that may occur on a bias edge. Using a single strand of regular sewing thread that has been knotted, take the first small running stitch, take a back stitch, then proceed with running stitches along the penciled line. End with a knot or a backstitch or two at the end of the penciled line. The seam allowances are free to be pressed in whatever direction seems appropriate, as we mention in Pressing. Because you have traced your pattern pieces accurately and they have not been subjected to any stretching under the presser foot of the machine, the result will be a neat and precise block. Press the block when it has been completed.

Another advantage to hand sewing is that it is portable: you can be piecing a block, while others are knitting or doing needlepoint.

MACHINE SEWING

Machine sewing is appealing to some quilters because it is faster. Assembly-line piecing is a viable alternative. Do remember to add the ¼-inch seam allowances to your templates if you plan to use your machine. Once your pieces have been traced and cut, you may safely stitch your seams using the ¼-inch guide on your machine. If your machine does not have a ¼-inch guideline, apply a strip of masking tape exactly ¼ inch from the needle and use it as your sewing guide.

"Chain piecing" (figure 1-1) is an invaluable aid to quiltmakers. If, for example, your block contains three triangles which are to be sewn to three squares, pin all of the combinations. Sew the first pair, but do not raise the presser foot or clip the thread. Instead, insert the next triangle/square combination and sew it, almost butting the edges of the first pair. Continue in this manner and you will have a series, or chain, of similar pairs. You have eliminated the wasted thread and wasted effort of removing each combination from beneath the presser foot. After the chain has been sewn, remove it from the machine and clip the connecting threads in order to release the individual units for the next step. Once you have mastered this technique, you will find many applications for it.

1-1. Chain piecing.

COMBINATION HAND AND MACHINE SEWING

In some designs it is possible to combine hand and machine sewing in one piece if you mark the ¼-inch sewing lines where needed. You may want to machine stitch long, straight seams, but hand sew slender points and sharp angles. Some quilt designs contain pieces with angles that require hand sewing. These pieces must be "set in." To do this, pin the first side of the angle to the piece it will join, matching pencil lines, and sew from the inner corner or point of the angle to the outside. Repeat this procedure on the adjacent seam line, always sewing from the point where the two seams meet to the outer edge. This eliminates any excess fabric from bunching up at the juncture of the two seams (figure 1-2).

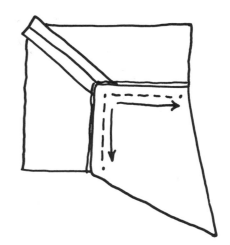

1-2. Setting in an angle.

PRESSING

The quiltmaking process requires pressing at several stages in order to achieve neat, professional-looking results. A good steam iron with a clean soleplate will make the job easier. However, as we mentioned in Fabrics and Fibers, it is essential to know the fiber content of the fabrics you are using so that you know how to treat them. If you are using 100% cottons, you can safely use your steam iron on its cotton setting; but, if you are using synthetics or blends, you should use a lower, perma-press setting. The cotton setting is too hot for these fabrics and will scorch them. With a combination of cottons and synthetics in one block, use the lower of the two settings.

Pressing should be done at four different times: 1). after the fabric has been washed, before cutting; 2). after the first seams have been sewn, but before others cross them; 3). when blocks are completed, and as they are joined; and 4). when the quilt or hanging is finished and ready to be layered.

In most instances seams should be pressed to one side, not open as with dressmaking. This adds strength to the seams (most important for a bed quilt) and is easier because the ¼-inch seams are difficult to press open without burning fingers. Occasionally, there are exceptions to this rule. For example, so many seams may come together at one point that pressing to one side would create a lump or thickness that will show on the front of the piece. If this happens, carefully press the seam open in order to minimize the bulk.

If you are using white or very light colors in your design, it is best to press the seams away from those pieces as often as possible. Sometimes, if this is not done, a dark thread or bit of seam allowance from a dark fabric will show through a light piece, resulting in an unattractive shadow on the front of the quilt. Always check for these stray threads before you begin the layering process.

Sometimes you will find that the design itself determines how it should be pressed. For example, if you are joining one row of squares to another row of squares, press the seams of the first row to the left and the seams of the second row to the right so that the joints meet smoothly and there is little bulk.

It is advisable to press very lightly from the wrong side to ensure that your seams are going in the proper direction. Do your final pressing, however, on the right side with the point of the iron so that you eliminate any folds or wrinkles in the seams.

While good pressing is essential, too much of a good thing can create other problems. Bias pieces can and will stretch, ripple, and change shape if overpressed. Long bias edges may be stay-stitched to avoid a potential problem, and an up/down press, gently resting the iron on the fabric instead of sliding and pulling should help. Most fabrics have a certain amount of "give" to them and can be stretched out of shape, although the straight, lengthwise grain is firmer than the crosswise grain of the fabric. Some of the wall hangings in this book contain large bias pieces, so it is especially important to press them carefully, but gently.

MARKING THE QUILT TOP

After you have pressed your sewn-together quilt top, it is time to decide where you will quilt. It is much easier to mark stitching lines on the quilt top at this point, rather than after layers have been fastened together.

You may wish simply to quilt the outlines of some or all of the pieces in your quilt. If so, there is no need to mark the quilt top. Just quilt ⅛ to ¼ inch inside or outside the seam lines around the desired shapes. On the other hand, if you choose to quilt other lines within, as opposed to around, the shapes, you will have to mark the right side of the quilt top in some way so that you can follow a line while you are stitching. A variety of marking devices are available for this purpose.

Special water-soluble markers are convenient and easy to use, and the marks disappear when dabbed with cold water. The advantage of this marker is the highly visible line that it produces. The disadvantage is the short life of this relatively costly device. A #3 lead pencil is also a good choice for marking on medium- or light-colored fabrics. The hard lead makes a very fine light line if the pencil is well sharpened. The slight shadows produced by quilting the surface of the quilt make the pencil marks almost invisible. A drawback to any lead pencil, however, is the danger of smudging, which, particularly on white fabric, could result in a grimy quilt. For dark fabrics, we find that an artist's white pencil is preferable to the soft tailor's chalk white pencil. Neither produces a line that can be easily removed, but the artist's pencil remains sharp longer and will give you a finer line.

Straight quilting lines can be marked using a yardstick or other straight edge as your pattern. For other designs, cardboard shapes may make good stencils, and there are also a large variety of commercial quilting stencils available in many sizes. You may also draw your own quilting design on paper with a black marker. Then slide the paper under the quilt top. If the fabric is a light color, you should be able to see the design well enough to trace it on the quilt top.

LAYERING

When the top of your quilt is completed and marked for quilting, the three layers (top, batting, and backing) must be fastened together in preparation for quilting.

It may be necessary to seam the backing fabric to make a sheet large enough for the back of your quilt. For example, perhaps the finished size of your quilt is 72 by 86 inches. Since the fabric you purchased for the quilt back is probably 45 inches wide, you will have to sew two widths of fabric together to accommodate the size of your quilt. There are several ways to do this, and your choice is just a matter of aesthetics. Whichever of the following methods you choose, it is very important to trim the selvage before sewing because the selvage will not have the same "give" as the rest of the fabric.

One way to seam the back is by simply sewing two pieces 45 inches wide by 86 inches long together along the lengthwise edges, creating a center seam down the backing (figure 1-3). The second method is similar to the first. Split one of the widths of fabric lengthwise, then stitch a half-width to each side of a full-width of fabric, creating two parallel lengthwise seams (figure 1-4). Both methods require about 5 yards of backing fabric for a 72- by 86-inch quilt, and you will end up with a sheet approximately 86 by 90 inches. Since this is far too wide for the quilt, you will have to trim the backing, thus wasting a good amount of fabric.

For this 72- by 86-inch quilt, an alternative, far more economical, method is to create a crosswise seam in the center of the backing. Simply sew two widths of 45- by 72-inch fabric to form a 72- by 89-inch (remember that you have trimmed away the selvage) sheet. This method requires only 4 yards of backing fabric (figure 1-5).

The choice of seaming for your quilt back is entirely up to you and will depend a great deal on the size of your quilt. Of course, any quilt or wall hanging that is less than 45 inches wide requires only one width of 45-inch fabric, in which case seaming is not necessary.

It is a good idea to set aside a whole day for the actual layering of your quilt, and sharing the task with a friend is even better. Find a flat surface large enough to accommodate the entire quilt. Usually the floor is the best choice, although a Ping-Pong table works well for some quilts. Place the backing right side down and tack or tape it along the edges to keep it from slipping. Next, lay the batting on top of the backing and smooth in place. Then place the top on the batting, right side up. A "sandwich" of backing, batting, and top is now in place. Allow a few inches of batting and backing to extend beyond the quilt top until you have completed your quilting and chosen your method of binding.

Beginning in the center of the quilt, pin all layers together in one hori-

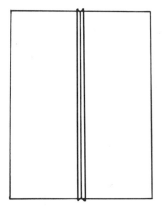

1-3. Method 1: sew together two pieces of backing fabric lengthwise to make one piece large enough for the quilt.

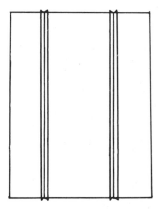

1-4. Method 2: sew a half-width of backing fabric to each side of a full width.

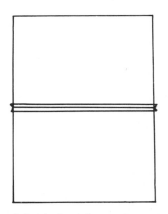

1-5. Method 3: sew two pieces of backing fabric together crosswise. This method is generally the most economical.

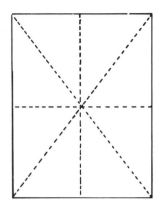

1-6. Start from the center and pin out to the sides, horizontally, vertically, and then diagonally.

1-7. Baste lines diagonally, then horizontally and vertically, across the entire quilt.

zontal line and then one vertical line, forming a cross. Next, pin a line from the center to each corner, forming an "X" (figure 1-6). As you pin, smooth any ripples gently toward the outside edges with your hand. Even the motion of pinning should be directed to the edge of the quilt with all the pins pointing in the direction in which you are heading. If the quilt is quite large, you may want to add a few additional rows of pins parallel to the first.

Basting is the next step. Use scrap thread, but avoid dusty, old spools or red or black thread (these all may leave little dots of color where you have stitched). Milliners' needles are excellent for basting because they are thin and very long.

Without knotting the end, thread the needle with a long single strand of thread. Begin at the center of the quilt, and, making sure the needle goes through all three layers, take 1- to 2-inch stitches to the outside edges. Leave a 2-inch tail of thread at each end of the line of basting so you can pull the threads out easily when you have finished quilting. First follow the pinned lines, then run rows of basting 5 inches apart horizontally and vertically, crisscrossing the quilt (figure 1-7). The object of the basting is to hold all the layers firmly together to avoid any shifting; so, the more basting you do, the more stable the layers will be to handle. If you flatten the quilt as much as possible in preparation for quilting, you will have no difficulty in creating a smoothly quilted surface. After basting is completed, remove pins.

QUILTING

It has become apparent to us during our years of teaching that even the most competent sewers first approach quilting apprehensively, with the assumption that they must adhere to well-defined rules. We are frequently asked questions about the "right" way to quilt, how a quilt "should" be quilted, and how many stitches to the inch are "required." Novice quilters feel that they should follow the same lines in terms of quantity, quality, and design as quilters have done for hundreds of years. Not so. That option is open to those of you who want to do so, but for those others of us whose busy lives preclude quarter-inch lines of parallel quilting, there are alternatives!

A quilt is, by definition, two layers of fabric with a filler or batting layered between the two. The three layers must be fastened together in some way in order to satisfy the definition. Our alternatives are to hand quilt, machine quilt, or tie, so that the layers function as one piece of fabric. The fastening together of the layers is functional, but it also serves a secondary purpose—that of enhancing the pieced or appliquéd quilt top with decorative stitching. Usually the quilting stitches serve both purposes.

HAND QUILTING

Hand quilting consists of small, running stitches that go through the three layers. Begin your quilting in the center of the piece and work toward the edges. Whether the quilt is to be stitched while in a hoop or frame, or just basted, the sewing hand works from the top while the other hand is used beneath the work to aid the upper hand in compressing the layers. The upper hand makes the stitches, controls their size, and pushes them through with the thimble. The needle pricks or grazes the index or middle finger of the lower hand. Most quilters take several stitches at a time before pushing the needle through, but there are proponents of the one-stitch-at-a-time method. A second thimble may be worn on the index or middle finger of the lower hand, so that it deflects each stitch taken by the upper hand and keeps it small and controlled (figure 1-8).

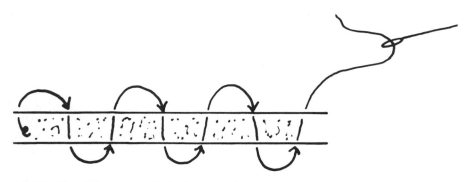

1-8. Hand quilting several stitches at a time.

Another single stitch method, called "stabbing," may be useful when quilting through extra seam allowances or heavy fabrics. The needle is inserted from top to bottom, then reinserted from bottom to the top to complete a stitch. The disadvantage to this method is that it is apt to produce uneven stitches on the underside of the quilt.

For all of these methods, begin and end the quilting as follows: tie a single knot and insert the needle a short distance from the first row of quilting, but only through the top layer. Give the thread a quick tug, and the knot will pull through the top surface layer and be concealed in the batting. End the quilting by tying a knot about ¼ inch from the surface, take a backstitch, and pull the knot through into the batting.

The size of the quilting stitches is another concern for beginning quilters. While we all strive for tiny, even stitches, it is often difficult to produce them because of the weight of the fabric or our own lack of expertise. Surface stitches that are five to nine to the inch are considered good, but there are variables. In the beginning it is more important to keep your stitches even than it is to worry about the number per inch. Quilting, like so many other manual skills, takes time, practice, and patience. The exaggerated up/down motion, which produces even stitches, will seem awkward at first, but that, too, will become easy and comfortable in time. Creating not only another design, but dimension, on an otherwise flat surface so enhances the piece that the novice quilter is usually encouraged to persevere.

We would hope to dispel any myths about any one method of quilting. We give you guidelines, but our teaching experience indicates that there are almost as many ways to quilt as there are quilters. A teacher, friend, or grandmother may provide the initial guidance, but usually these instructions are modified and the quilter develops his or her own technique.

MACHINE QUILTING

Machine quilting is the alternative to hand quilting. The preparation of the layers is the same, although special emphasis must be placed on the amount of basting. Extra basting is important because the piece has to be able to fit under the presser foot of a machine, which makes it impossible to use a hoop or frame. Heavy pinning, as the work is quilted from the center to the sides, is also helpful. Stitching may be done "in the ditch," within the seamlines, to conceal it, producing a puffy look, or it may follow decorative design lines. Working from the center out on a piece is most important. The pressure of the presser foot on the three layers often causes the layers to shift and creates wrinkles and bunches if done in the reverse manner. It is also important to check the tension of the machine on a sample piece. Sometimes, loosening the tension eliminates some of the "shift" but requires the sewer to exercise greater control in manipulating the quilt. Machine quilting is not appropriate for a very large piece, but may be effectively done on a small quilt, both in terms of function and aesthetics.

Because wall quilts are smaller and will not be subjected to repeated washings and daily use, they need not necessarily be quilted as heavily as bed quilts. The sturdiness of the polyester batting that we use allows us to quilt sparsely if a flat, nonsculptured look is desired. There are opponents to today's overabundance of synthetics, but certainly early quiltmakers would join with us in recognizing synthetic batting as a boon to our craft. There is no longer the need for such quantities of intricate quilting because the sturdiness of the batting allows for larger areas to be left unquilted. When the quilting design can contribute artistically, instead of out of necessity, there is greater opportunity for creative expression.

TYING

Quilt layers may be fastened together with small ties, a method that is sometimes referred to as "tufting." The ties may be of crochet string, perle cotton, buttonhole twist, or yarn.

To tie a quilt, thread a large needle with a length of one of these strings. Take a stitch through the three layers from the top, then take a second stitch in the same place. Tie the string in a square knot and cut the ends about 1 inch from the surface of the quilt.

Plan to tie your quilt at evenly spaced intervals (for instance, where the blocks join and in the centers of the blocks). The ties should not be more than 5 or 6 inches apart so that the quilt is strong enough to withstand laundering and use. The color of the string may be one that is used in the quilt or it may be a contrasting one.

Tying is suitable for bed quilts if you like the appearance of the ties, but we do not recommend it for wall quilts. We feel that the ties would detract from the designs, and we prefer the added dimension that hand quilting provides.

BINDING

Binding adds the finishing touch to your quilt. It outlines the boundaries of the piece and, at the same time, finishes the edges. The two most common ways to bind a quilt are: 1). separate binding using long strips of fabric to conceal the raw edge; or 2). self-binding, which is done by turning an extension of either the quilt top or backing over the raw edge and hemming it down.

Each method has its strong points. Self-binding is quick; it can be accomplished completely by machine. A separate binding can align a slightly crooked quilt, and it can be replaced when the margins of the quilt begin to show signs of wear. Function (is the piece for bed or wall?) and appearance (will it have a wide border, narrow border, no border?) determine which method to use.

SEPARATE BINDING

Recently, commercial quilt bindings have become available, but many of us choose to make our own binding anyway, because we feel restricted by the limited color range of the packaged product. Making separate binding is easy and can be accomplished in almost as little time as it takes to read about it. But first let us free ourselves of that conditioned association between bias and binding. Quilt bindings are not cut on the bias (diagonal to the straight grain of the fabric) unless the quilt is shaped with scallops or curves along the edges. By its nature, bias is very stretchy and it conforms to the curves easily. When binding straight edges, you will find elasticity a handicap.

A separate binding is cut in long strips on the grain of the fabric. The lengthwise grain is preferable because it does not stretch as much as the crossgrain, and it can be cut continuously to any measurement, so that the binding can be made without seams. In a bed quilt, seams in the binding are inconspicuous, but a wall quilt is often at eye level and it is best to try to avoid seams here. However, when you find yourself with a 72-inch quilt to bind and a yard of fabric to do the job, the choice is seams. Make them less obvious by adjusting your machine to sew the seams at about twenty stitches per inch. Normal machine sewing is done at about twelve stitches per inch. The increased density makes for a smoother, flatter seam.

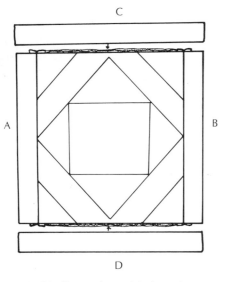

1-9. Binding strips added to the quilt.

Several sewing-machine manufacturers now make an attachment called an even-feed foot. This attachment feeds the top layer of fabric through the machine at the same rate as the bottom layer. It is particularly useful in sewing on bindings because it prevents fabric from slipping under the needle, which causes puckers or wrinkles.

Quilt binding is not an estimated or "guesstimated" process; binding should be cut to the actual measurements in your quilt plan. Some beginning quilters approach binding by cutting a long continuous strip, sewing it on, and then snipping off the leftover strip at the end of each side. When you choose to apply unmeasured binding this way, you are losing your last opportunity to bring the quilt into true alignment. Fabrics in the quilt top can stretch during piecing and, despite block-by-block corrections, there can be some distortion in the finished quilt. If your finished top is distorted, self-binding would be a poor choice because it does not allow for *truing up*, as does separate binding.

The binding strips should be cut 1½ inches wide. This includes ¼-inch seam allowances. The length is determined by the size of the quilt. To add binding strips to your quilt follow these steps:

1. Calculate the length of binding Strips A and B (figure 1-9) according to the measurements in your quilt plan, adding ¼ inch to each end of the strips for seam allowances. Mark this point in pencil. Leave a little extra (about 1 inch) beyond this mark to allow for human error and miscalculations.

2. Right sides together, pin Strips A and B to the front sides of the quilt. Start pinning at the pencil lines you have made at each end of the strips. Then pin the center and the quarter points. Pin generously between these points to distribute the fabric evenly along the binding strip.

3. Sew along the ¼-inch seam lines. Trim the excess.

4. Determine the length of Strips C and D (figure 1-9) from your quilt plan.

5. Pin and sew C and D onto the quilt. Once you have added the bindings (figures 1-10a-10d) you are ready to fold the edges and stitch the binding in place.

6. Turn under ¼ inch along the length of A and B (figure 1-10c).

7. Fold A and B along the edge of the trimmed quilt and pin.

8. Sew in place with a blindstitch (figure 1-11).

9. Turn under ¼ inch along C and D.

10. Fold C and D along the edge of the quilt and blind stitch in place.

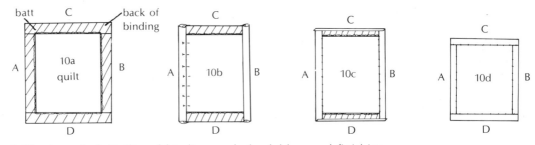

1-10a through d. Quilt and binding ready for folding and finishing.

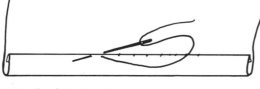

1-11. The blindstitch.

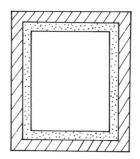

1-12. The quilt is trimmed and ready for mitered corners using the quilt backing. Dots indicate the extended batting. Diagonal lines indicate the wrong side of the quilt backing.

INVISIBLE BINDING

This method uses separate binding strips that do not show in the front of the finished quilt. **Easter** and **Perpetual Motion** were bound in this way.

1. Trim batt and backing flush with the quilt front.
2. Cut the binding strips 1 inch wide. Calculate the binding lengths, pin and sew exactly as described under Separate Binding above.
3. Turn under ¼ inch and bring the remaining ½ inch to the back of the quilt. Pin.
4. Blindstitch to the back of the quilt.
5. Repeat for sides C and D, folding the corners neatly.

SELF-BINDING WITH THE QUILT BACKING

The quilt can be bound by bringing the backing fabric around to the top and stitching it down.

1. Trim the batt to extend beyond the quilt top. If you plan to have a 1½-inch binding, allow the batt to extend 1½ inches beyond the seam line.
2. Cut the backing 3¼ inches beyond the seam line. This allows enough fabric to cover the front and back of the 1½-inch batt extension plus a ¼-inch hem. If you have used a thick batt, allow an extra ¼ inch to accommodate this thickness. Use Steps 1 and 2 for any binding width you choose.

For finishing and hemming, use the directions for folding and finishing given for Separate Bindings or use the following directions for mitering the corners.

MITERING THE CORNERS

In order to make very neat corners, mitering is often recommended. To miter corners, follow these directions.

1. Prepare the quilt so that the batting extends beyond the quilt top as shown in figure 1-12 and the backing fabric extends beyond the batting on all sides as described above.
2. Fold a corner down so the tip comes to the seam line (figure 1-13a).
3. Fold the tip under or cut it off so it will not be visible later (figure 1-13b).
4. Turn under ¼ inch along the edges of the two adjacent sides A and C (figure 1-13b).

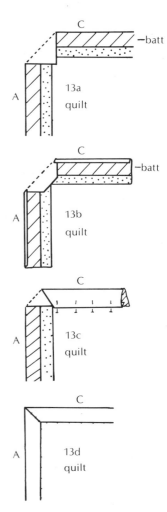

1-13a through d. Mitering the corner.

5. Fold side C down over the batt, bringing it to the seam line. Pin (figure 1-13c).

6. Repeat along side A, adjusting the corner. Pin.

7. Repeat these steps for all corners.

8. Blindstitch (figure 1-11) along the pinned edges and stitch the mitered edges together (figure 1-13d).

SELF-BINDING WITH THE QUILT FRONT

This binding method is the reverse of the self-binding with the quilt backing. Use the instructions for Self-Binding with the Quilt Backing. Remember, however, that this requires an extended border on the quilt *front* which is folded over the raw edges and sewn onto the quilt back.

THE END RESULTS

How you will proceed from here will depend upon how you intend to display your quilt—as a bed covering or as a hanging on your wall. Displaying the quilt is such an important aspect of quiltmaking that we decided to devote all of Chapter 2 to that subject.

2

Bed Quilts and Wall Quilts

Beds have been the time-honored place to display quilts and, although we prefer to hang our quilts, certainly we appreciate this tradition. When we make bed quilts we have several practical concerns that we don't have to consider when making less practical wall quilts.

PRACTICAL CONSIDERATIONS FOR BED QUILTS

First, bed quilts need to be sturdy. Whether made by hand or machine, a bed quilt needs to be constructed with utility in mind. There are many, many seams in a patchwork quilt. That means there are many, many places for stitches to come loose or unravel. Once the three layers have been quilted, it is very hard to repair a seam. So, as we have detailed throughout this book, careful construction and good materials are essential.

Second, we like to make bed quilts that can be washed at home rather than ones that must be brought to the dry cleaners. This means planning ahead. All the materials in the quilt must be washable and colorfast. The fabrics should be prewashed to determine whether they are.

As far as maintenance is concerned, it is better to wash a quilt before it gets very dirty. It is, of course, much easier to clean a lightly soiled quilt;

the rigorous agitation necessary to get out heavy dirt is injurious to the fabrics in a quilt.

If you choose to wash your quilt by machine, fill the washer's tub with lukewarm water. Following the manufacturer's directions, *thoroughly* dissolve mild soap in the water. Put the quilt into the washer and run the gentle cycle—for not more than six minutes of agitation. Rinse the quilt at least twice to remove all traces of soap. Allow the quilt to spin only long enough to remove most of the water.

If you want to hand wash your quilt, you will need a large tub. For all practical purposes, the bathtub is the usual choice. Fill the tub with lukewarm water. Following the manufacturer's directions, thoroughly dissolve an amount of mild soap in the tub. Stir to distribute the soap evenly throughout the water. Fold the quilt into the water, accordion-fashion, and let it soak for a few minutes. Then, using your hands, squeeze the soapy water through the quilt, working evenly over the whole surface. Drain the water. Press the water out of the quilt with your hands, or wring very gently, being careful not to snap the quilting stitches. Fill the tub with lukewarm, clear water. Rinse the quilt. Repeat the rinse process, pressing out as much water as possible. If it is at all practical, roll the quilt in terry towels, as this will remove water more gently than wringing. This procedure is very hard on your body, and it takes more time than most people would care to spend on an unpleasant activity. For that reason we try to make our bed-sized quilts small enough to fit into a washing machine.

An automatic dryer is good for drying quilts because it will fluff up the batting while drying the quilt. Do not use a hot dryer. The "warm" or "air only" setting is best.

If your quilt is tied or has large unquilted areas, there is nothing to prevent the batting from shifting around inside the quilt during washing. Prevention of this disaster is much easier than a cure. Temporarily fasten the three layers together every three or four inches over the whole surface. Do this by using rust-proof safety pins, or by basting with thread. Wash and dry as usual, and remove the pins or basting before putting the quilt back on the bed.

Quilts can be made any size you wish, but most people make either a bedspread or a coverlet. A bedspread is wide enough to cover the mattress and box springs, and long enough to cover the pillows. A coverlet is wide enough to cover the mattress, and, sometimes, but not always, long enough to cover the pillows. There are some benefits to restricting bed quilts to the coverlet size. A small quilt is easy to care for; it can fit comfortably into an automatic washer. Small quilts are easy to store. They use less fabric and are more quickly made than to-the-floor bed covers. Many of the designs presented here as wall quilts can be elaborated with a few borders; this will make them large enough to cover the top and sides of a mattress. Small quilts can be used over a plain-colored bedspread for decorative beauty and warmth.

Dust ruffles are good quilt "extenders" for coverlets. Many beautiful dust ruffles are available ready-made, but they can be made from fabric that coordinates with your quilt. A purchased dust ruffle can be customized by sewing on a 1-inch band of quilt fabric about 4 inches up from the floor. Pillow shams, quilted or unquilted, can be used with your coverlet.

When it is not in use, a quilt can be folded at the bottom of the bed, or folded over a quilt stand. Commercial quilt stands are available in brass or wood, some even as do-it-yourself kits. Sometimes you may not want to spread, drape, or fold your quilt. You may want to hang it on the wall.

DISPLAYING YOUR WALL QUILT

Hanging a quilt is a lot like framing a picture. If it is well done, it enhances the piece in a very subtle way. On the other hand, if you notice the frame before you notice the picture, then the frame is not doing its job. In a similar way, a well-mounted quilt appears to have no visible means of support. The mounting devices are totally unobtrusive, yet the quilt is evenly supported and shown to its best advantage. Conversely, haphazard mounting can take a terrible toll even from masterpiece quilts. Ripples and sags cannot be ignored. They cast unflattering shadows and draw attention away from design and craftsmanship.

Recently, there was a juried quilt show in Hartford, Connecticut. The museum curator was an imaginative professional with an appreciation for the art and craft of quilting. Outstanding examples of both old and new quilts were carefully selected, and everyone felt confident that the show would be impressive. But, as the quilts came in, our stalwart curator developed a few headaches. The problem was not the quilts. They were even more beautiful than anticipated, and the craftsmanship was flawless. The problem was that many of the quilts were very poorly prepared for display. A masterpiece quilt arrived with a hank of used clothesline and twenty-seven large safety pins. Presumably these were to be used to hang the quilt. A solid-color wall quilt clearly displayed the lumpy ridge of its supporting dowel along with some exquisite quilting. A wall quilt shaped with sharp geometric extensions drooped along its points and lost much of its dramatic appeal as a result.

The curator coped well beyond the reaches of his job and the show was a big success, but there are a few lessons to be learned here. One is that preparation for display is always the quilter's responsibility. All too often, the people who are hanging the show have to go to extraordinary measures to see that a quilt looks all right when hanging. Another is that it is possible to mount *all* quilts successfully no matter how oddly shaped. Preparing and mounting simple rectangles or squares is downright easy. The information in this section will show you several methods of hanging quilts, one of which is sure to work for you, whether your quilt will be hung in a museum, a quilt show, or on your wall at home.

33

MOUNTING TECHNIQUES

The many techniques for hanging quilts can be divided into two broad categories—hard (or rigid) mounting and soft mounting. The former method involves the use of artists' wooden stretchers or similar devices so that the quilt is held firmly on all sides. Sometimes a hard-mounted piece is actually framed with a wood or metal frame. Soft mounting allows the quilt to hang freely against the wall. Only the top is supported, usually by a wooden firring strip (lattice) through a casing on the back of the quilt. Neither method is inherently better than the other, but the one you choose will make a difference in the way your quilt looks.

Hard mounting tends to give the quilt a formal appearance. The quilt is held stiffly all around. Since people have been conditioned to think of quilts as soft, when they come upon a rigid one it catches them a little off guard; they tend to look twice at a piece that is hard mounted.

If your finished quilt does not cooperate by lying flat against the wall, hard mounting is an excellent way to solve the problem. Little wrinkles and sags can be stretched away. A recalcitrant rectangle or square can be coaxed back into shape over a stretcher with a little sleight of hand and a few well-placed staples.

Hard mounting is more time consuming than soft mounting, and it can be expensive. If you have access to a well-equipped workshop, you may be able to make your own stretchers and/or frames. We have had good experiences with frame-it-yourself shops in our area, and we would recommend relying on their supplies, help, and advice. Stretchers and some packaged frames can be purchased at art-supply stores. If money is not a concern you can bring your quilt to be mounted at a professional framing shop. Keep in mind that few professional framers have had experience mounting quilts, so it is best to know ahead exactly how you want your quilt to look. Give the framer as much specific information as you can, trying to be sure that you both have the same end result in mind.

Soft mounting has its own advantages. It is fast and cheap and can be done completely at home. The only unusual item needed is a wooden firring strip, readily available at building suppliers or lumberyards. This lattice can be removed from its casing easily, and the quilt can then be folded or rolled for storage or transportation.

A soft-mounted quilt is less controversial. It looks appropriately tractable. The quilt hangs soft and free against the wall. The low-relief sculptural dimension formed by the quilting stitches is more evident than in a hard-mounted piece because the surface is not stretched flat.

Many of our students have made bed quilts that they show occasionally at fairs and quilt shows. A casing can be made of the same fabric as the backing and it will be inconspicuous when the quilt is in use. At show time, a lattice can be slipped into the casing and the quilt will display much better than if it had been push-pinned.

In this section you will find all the step-by-step information you need to try several variations of both hard and soft mounting. We also include methods to help you with hard-to-hang quilts.

CASING

This method involves sewing a casing or sleeve to the back of the quilt to accommodate a wooden firring strip (lattice). If your quilt is less than 50 inches wide, a single sleeve will be adequate. Beyond this length, it is better to make two separate sleeves, allowing space between them for additional support (figure 2-1).

Materials

1 wooden firring strip, cut 2 inches narrower than the quilt
3-inch-wide fabric strip, length depends on quilt
2 or 3 small screw eyes

Procedure

1. Cut a fabric strip 3 inches wide by the desired finished length of the sleeve plus ½ inch. Remember that you will want to end the casing about 1 inch or so from the edge so the wooden strip will not show in front.
2. Turn under a ¼ inch seam at each end of the strip and stitch down by hand or machine.
3. Baste or iron under ¼-inch across the top and bottom of the strip.
4. Center and pin this across the top of the quilt about ½ inch down from the top edge (figure 2-1).
5. Blind stitch in place.
6. Cut the wooden strip to the desired length and sand.
7. Add small screw eyes in the wooden strip or drill holes for hanging. If you find that your quilt is not lying flat against the wall, you can add another casing along the bottom and insert another wooden strip.

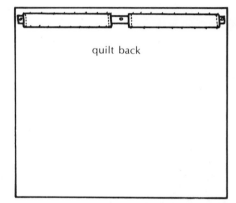

quilt back

2-1. View of quilt back with casings.

VELCRO

This is a useful technique for hanging smaller pieces.

Materials

1 wooden firring strip, cut 2 inches narrower than the quilt.
Velcro, 2 inches narrower than the quilt
staple gun or special Velcro glue
a drill or small screw eyes

Procedure

1. Sew one piece of the Velcro to the quilt back, about ½ inch from the top.

2. Staple or glue the companion piece of Velcro onto the wooden strip.

3. Drill holes in the wooden strip or put screw eyes into the strip for hanging.

4. Press the two Velcro strips together. Hang by stringing the holes in the wooden strip with invisible nylon line; or, hammer two headless nails into the wall aligned with the holes in the strip. To hang, set the headless nails into the holes.

BANNER METHOD

In this method the hanging solution is part of the design. The loops can be used on the top and bottom, as in **Medicine Man** (see page 78) or on the top only (figure 2-2). The size, spacing, and number of loops depends on the size of the quilt. Try not to leave large spaces between the loops or the quilt will gape.

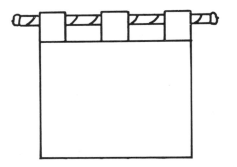

2-2. Quilt hanging like a banner with loops on the top.

Materials

fabric that appears in the quilt or one that complements it
dowel(s) or rod(s)

Procedure

1. Cut long fabric strips twice as wide as the desired finished loop width, plus ½ inch for seam allowances.

2. Fold fabric in half lengthwise, keeping the right sides together.

3. Sew down the length, allowing a ¼-inch seam. You now have a tube (figure 2-3). Turn this to the right side and iron flat with the seam in the center back.

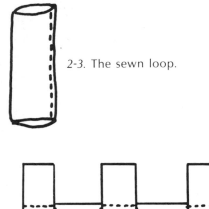

2-3. The sewn loop.

4. To cut the loop lengths, double the desired finished loop length and add an extra inch or so. Make sure each loop is exactly the same length.

5. Fold each loop in half. To eliminate the raw edges, you can finish the ends with a zigzag stitch on the machine, with a whip stitch by hand, or by turning under a ¼-inch hem on each end of the tube.

6. Attach the loops to the back of the quilt by hand (figure 2-4), making sure that the distance from the top of the quilt to the top of the loop is uniform. Space the loops evenly across the top of the quilt.

7. Insert rod. Set rod on headless nails to hang.

8. Optional loops at the bottom may be added in the same manner.

back

2-4. Attach the loops to the back of the quilt.

METAL FRAMES

This method is best for pieces 36 inches or less (see **Interstices,** page 90). If you are lucky enough to have finished measurements that conform to the precut, packaged metal frames available in chrome or gold color, the cost of your frame will be less than if you need a custom-cut frame. The metal frames available from frame shops are more costly but are available in a wide variety of colors and can be cut to any dimensions. These frames have a channel that holds the mounted quilt in place.

Materials

foam board (available at art-supply stores; it is lightweight and has no adverse effects on fabric.)
2 ½- to 3-inch-wide tape (e.g., aluminum duct tape)
metal frame (order the frame after the piece is mounted on the foamboard so you will have the exact measurements.)

Procedure

1. If your quilt design has points that extend to the outer edges, rather than a border, it will be necessary to add a 2-inch border strip to all four sides. This will provide enough fabric to be wrapped around to the back.
2. To determine the measurements of the foamboard, use the dimensions for the finished piece given on the project page and add ½ inch for stretching and seam allowances. Cut a piece of foamboard to this size. The outer points of the quilt should end ¼ inch from the edge of the foamboard when the piece is stretched slightly so the frame does not cover the points. Too much pressure from stretching will bend the foamboard and cause it to pop out of the frame.
3. Stretch opposite sides and tape down on the back of the foamboard. Check the front periodically to see that you are not distorting the pattern.
4. After the mounting is done, place long strips of the wide tape across the raw edges on the back to give it a clean look.
5. Purchase a metal frame for these dimensions. Assemble and hang.

STRETCHER FRAMES

This method works best for quilts no larger than about 48 inches (see **Skyscrapers,** page 87). Stretchers are wooden slats that interlock at the ends. They are available in any desired length at art-supply stores (figure 2-5).

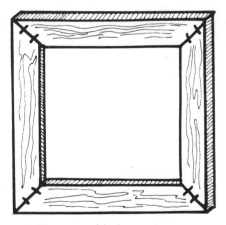

2-5. The assembled stretcher.

Materials

stretchers to fit the finished dimensions of your quilt
staple gun
picture wire
screw eyes
mat board, the same size as the stretcher, to be used to cover the back (optional)

37

Procedure

1. Be sure that your quilt has enough border fabric on the front to extend to the back, covering the stretcher. Finished edges make the piece look better from the back, but they are optional.

2. Center the assembled stretcher on the back of the quilt.

3. Working from the back, and, starting in the center, staple opposing sides of the border fabric to the stretcher, keeping the work taut and checking frequently to be sure the design is not askew (figure 2-6).

4. Finish the corners (figures 2-7, 2-8).

5. If you wish, staple the mat board over the back of the work.

6. Insert two small screw eyes into the wood of the stretcher about one-third of the way down from the top. String picture wire between the screw eyes and hang (figure 2-9).

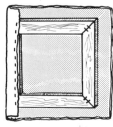 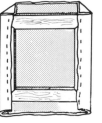 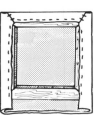 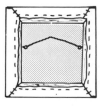

2-6. Staple left side to stretcher.

2-7. Turn under corners.

2-8. Fold top down over stretcher and staple.

2-9. Finished view of back, showing placement of screw eyes and picture wire for hanging.

STRETCHER WITH FABRIC FRAME

This is similar to the above method, except that, before stretching, the quilt is finished with a ½-inch binding. This binding extends beyond the stretcher, like corded piping on a pillow, creating a fabric frame for the piece (figure 2-10). Separate strips of fabric are sewn to the back of the quilt to attach the quilt to the stretcher. **Sunlight Through the Trees** is finished this way.

Materials

stretchers to fit the finished quilt dimensions, minus ½ inch on each side to allow the binding to extend
staple gun
½ yard (¾ yard for quilts over 44 inches) of the same fabric you used to bind your quilt

Procedure

1. Finish your quilt with a binding which shows ½ inch on the front. Self-binding by machine is particularly good here (see page 29). The back of your quilt will look like figure 2-11.

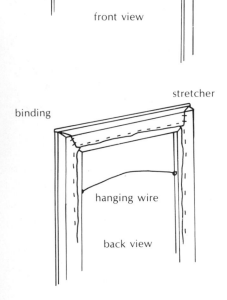

binding

stretcher

finished quilt front

front view

stretcher

binding

hanging wire

back view

2-10. Front and back views of a quilt finished with a *fabric frame*.

2. From the ½ yard of binding fabric, cut four strips, each 2½ inches wide. Piecing, if necessary, make each strip the length of each side, plus 4 inches. For example, if your quilt measures 36 inches by 48 inches, cut two strips 40 inches, and two strips 52 inches.

3. Leaving 2 inches extra at each end, pin one strip (hereafter called Strip A) to the back of the quilt, with the right side of the strip against the back of the quilt. The inner raw edge of Strip A extends ¼ inch beyond the binding seam. Figure 2-12 shows an X-ray view of this procedure.

4. From the right side, stitch in the ditch directly on top of the binding seam. Be sure to sew carefully because this line of stitching will show (figure 2-13). Back tack at the beginning and the end of each side. Remove pins.

5. Sew strips on the other three sides in the same manner. They will meet, but not join, in the corners. Do not cut the extra 2 inches off the ends.

6. Center assembled stretcher on the back of the quilt, having the edges of the stretcher flush with the binding seam.

7. Place Strip A over the stretcher and staple (figure 2-14). Finish corners as follows: cover the wooden corner of the stretcher with the 2-inch extension of Strip A, by folding the raw edge smoothly to the back of the stretcher (see arrow, figure 2-14). Fold back the extra fabric on Strip B (figure 2-15). Fold Strip B into a triangle (figure 2-16). Then fold Strip B down over the stretcher and staple. The finished joint is shown in the back view of figure 2-10.

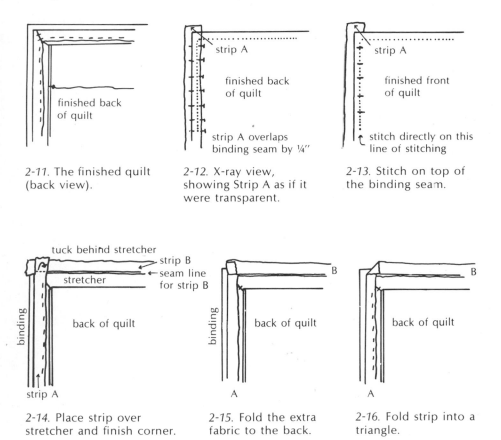

2-11. The finished quilt (back view).

2-12. X-ray view, showing Strip A as if it were transparent.

2-13. Stitch on top of the binding seam.

2-14. Place strip over stretcher and finish corner.

2-15. Fold the extra fabric to the back.

2-16. Fold strip into a triangle.

8. Repeat for the other three sides.

9. Insert screw eyes in the wood of the stretcher. String with picture wire and hang.

CONTOUR CASINGS

This method involves making casings that are shaped to the contours of the quilt.

Materials

3-inch-wide bias strips of fabric
plexiglass or masonite, ¼ inch thick

Procedure

1. Cut 3-inch-wide bias strips and follow the instructions for making casings on page 35. Use short pieces of the bias strips matching the contours of the quilt back.

2. Cut a piece of plexiglass or masonite 1½ inches wide to match the shape of the casings.

3. Find the center of the plexiglass or masonite form and drill a hole.

4. Sand the edges.

5. Slip through the loops and hang. If you use masonite, place the finished smooth side toward the quilt (figure 2-17).

WOODEN ARMATURES

This is similar to the soft hanging method described under the heading Velcro. Here, however, the wood support is cut to reflect the shape of the quilt.

Materials

Velcro
staple gun or Velcro glue
¼-inch plywood
handsaw
a drill or small screw eyes

Procedure 1

1. Using ¼-inch plywood, cut an armature approximately 2 inches wide that follows the contours of the upper portion of the quilt and extends out to the widest part of it (figure 2-18). The armature should be somewhat smaller than the quilt so it will not protrude beyond the edges and be visible from the front.

2. Staple or glue one side of the Velcro strip to the plywood armature.

3. Sew the companion piece of Velcro to the corresponding part of the back of the quilt, about ½ inch in from the edges.

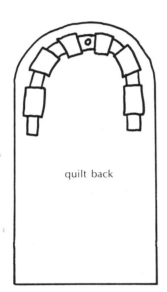

2-17. Contour casings attached to the back of the quilt.

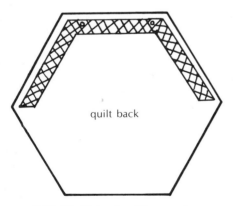

2-18. Quilt back with wooden armature ready to hang.

4. Drill two holes into the plywood armature or add small screw eyes for hanging.

5. Press corresponding pieces of Velcro together to secure the quilt to the armature.

Note: If you want a rigid appearance, the armature can be extended around the entire perimeter of the piece. Cut out the center of the plywood to reduce the weight and to keep the fabric from touching the wood.

You can use a modified form of this technique to hang even the most peculiar shapes. Sketch the shape of the quilt on paper and try to figure out what would be the most supportive way to form the armature (figure 2-19).

Procedure 2

1. Cut the armature out of ¼-inch plywood.

2. Figure out where the Velcro would provide the most support and staple or glue it in place.

3. Sew the corresponding pieces of Velcro to the quilt back in the same places that the Velcro appears on the armature (figure 2-20).

4. Drill holes in the armature or put in small screw eyes for hanging on wire or headless nails.

5. Press the armature to the quilt back and hang.

2-19. Wooden armature with Velcro for unconventional quilt shape.

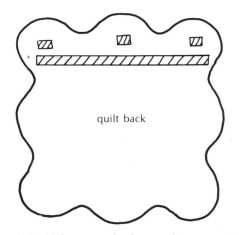

2-20. Velcro attached to quilt corresponds to placement of Velcro on the armature.

3

The
Art of
Quiltmaking

Sometimes the prospect of designing a pattern is very exhilarating, but, when the tools are assembled, that blank piece of paper can be very intimidating. An elusive tool called "creativity" is necessary and it isn't sitting on the table. There are no patterns or pictures to use as guides, no antique quilts to copy.

All children are creative, but many adults have lost confidence in their ability to create; and so, uncultivated, that ability atrophies. To overcome this lack of confidence or fear of failure we have to take certain risks. We enter a phase in which we feel less secure, but, once we pass through this stage, we feel great joy and pleasure in the creation of our designs. The experience is self-perpetuating.

Inspiration comes at odd times, in strange places, and often when we least expect it—in the middle of the night, while sitting in a meeting, riding a train, or walking the dog. Just as it is impossible to sit with your mind completely blank, it is impossible not to absorb the beauty of nature, as well as the graphics in an advertisement, a piece of fabric, food packaging, a mosaic tile, or an art exhibit. Try to keep a notebook of ideas, color combinations, visual impressions of something that you may someday want to interpret in fabric. Sometimes ideas seem wonderful at the moment, but they lose their appeal the next day or week. Others resurface much later, having redeemed themselves, and become exciting pieces. When we leave our minds open to these visual stimuli that surround us, the creative process has already begun, and the task of interpreting the inspiration and putting it on paper is fun. It is our hope that, in addition to using the designs we've presented in this book, you go on to designing your own quilt patterns, as well.

Since the creative process differs from one person to the next, the rest of this chapter will deal with our individual approaches and techniques. Perhaps you will find that you identify with one person and will follow her procedure. Most likely, you will try different techniques, adapt parts of each method, and then develop your own style.

AN APPROACH TO DESIGN: SARAH DOOLAN GOBES

The quiltmakers I have met are either artists who have discovered that fabric provides them with a new and interesting medium, or lifelong sewers who have the skills and want to use them in a more artistic way. (I have never met a quiltmaker who did not fall into one or the other of these two categories, although I am sure that one must exist.)

I grew up in a family of artists *and* sewers. The artists' credentials were intimidating, so I avoided art courses, but sewing satisfied the creative urge. I progressed from doll clothes, aprons, and dirndl skirts to more difficult garments, and I remained on this plateau for years. A book club selection on quilting inspired me to break out of my "holding pattern" and try something new. Its arrival coincided with the birth of a friend's baby, which provided both the need and the inspiration for my first quilt. I stitched together pastel squares, tied and bound the quilt and have been making quilts ever since.

At first, I concentrated on executing traditional pieced patterns; they were beautiful and their geometry fascinated me. The supply of them was endless, and these draftings provided me with invaluable lessons in the mathematics of quiltmaking. Once I understood that concept, progressing to original designs seemed very logical. I took basic geometric shapes and divided them as did the early quiltmakers. I found the translation to fabric of an original design rewarding and satisfying.

Drafting a new pattern is one of my favorite steps in the quiltmaking process. The tools are quite simple: I keep on hand a supply of graph paper pads in different sized grids, as well as rulers, pencils, an indispensable T-square, and a set of felt-tipped markers in many colors.

I usually begin by outlining a square on graph paper. I then draw or connect lines until "something happens." This can be approached with an open mind, much like doodling, but I often have some idea in mind before I start. For my "bird" block I divided the square into four equal sections. Then I divided three of them on the diagonal (figure 3-1). To form the tail I drew lines from the midpoints of the borders of the small blank square to the central intersection. The addition of four more diagonal lines gave the bird some wings and a head (figure 3-2). To complete the block I added parallel lines, midpoint to midpoint, on the three corner triangles (figure 3-3). The bird exists without these lines, but these add design interest when several "bird" blocks are joined.

When the resulting design seems interesting, I add more blocks to see if

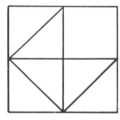

3-1. To create the "bird" block, start by dividing a square into four parts, then dividing three of them on the diagonal.

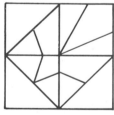

3-2. Draw lines as shown to create the tail, wings, and head.

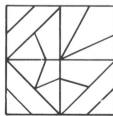

3-3. Enhance the design by drawing parallel lines as shown.

43

the secondary design, that which appears when several blocks are added to one another, is attractive. Sometimes that secondary design does not appear, in which case the block must be strong enough to stand by itself. I seldom rework a block that does not appeal to me. I prefer to start with a fresh piece of graph paper and a new idea.

If a design seems to have possibilities, I draft it to scale, using one square on the graph paper grid per inch in the final piece. I add as many blocks as I think I might use in the quilt or wall hanging. At this point I start to experiment with colors, first adding the strongest color, the part of the design that I wish to emphasize. First I made the birds the strongest color, either dark or bright, so that they would stand out (figure 3-4). Next the squares and half-squares were shaded with the predominant color, which would be interesting if done on a large quilt or hanging (figure 3-5). Then I put the background shapes (all those that are not birds or squares) in the strongest color—the birds and squares appear to be super-imposed on the dark background (figure 3-6). I feel that this is a useful exercise for the beginner and expert alike. These illustrations show, rather dramatically, how the use of different color values can change the appearance of a design.

3-4. The part of the design that is done in the strongest color is the part that will be emphasized. Here the birds stand out the most.

3-5. With this use of color the squares and half-squares stand out.

3-6. The background is emphasized here.

There are times when I have a specific color in mind. It may be a color I've not worked with recently, or perhaps I have seen a fabric that I would like to use *because* of its color. The piece may be intended for a specific room—a bedroom or a wall in a den—a place where the main color may be dictated by the other furnishings. I like colors, both the clear, bright ones and also the muted shades, but I do get bored with too much of one. If I have just finished a project in blues, I must allow the color blue to take a temporary rest, both in my head and on the shelf. When this happens I am eager to work with yellow or brown—any color but blue. I am always changing the colors I work with to keep myself interested and to keep my pieces from looking alike.

I am fortunate to have a sewing room that I can call my own. It is a room where I can leave the mess and not feel the need to apologize to guests. I work on a very large plywood table that allows space for a sewing machine and tools, as well as room to cut and design. My fabrics are kept in plastic bags, grouped by color. A bulletin board holds design ideas, swatches of fabric, and notes to myself. A plexiglass cookbook holder works well for supporting a pad of graph paper while a new design is being studied. My large white walls are perfect for hanging works in progress so that I can stand back and see how the piece looks from a distance. This is important; so often it is necessary to get a different perspective.

There are times when working in this space of mine, whether at night or on a sunny morning, is enough to provide me with sufficient inspiration to create a design. Perhaps ideas have been floating around in my head and the very act of sitting down with my tools provides me with the stimulation I need. On occasion, something external provides the inspiration— on the day after an ice storm, the trees are rigid and, when the sun's rays shine on them, they produce strange and interesting angles. Regardless of where my ideas come from, I do know that the time I spend alone, when it is quiet and I can plan a new design, is my favorite part of the whole process. Occasionally, it is difficult to achieve the exact results I had envisioned. Those designs will likely remain in a notebook and will never appear on a wall or bed. The creation of a design that "works" and demands to be stitched is very exciting and satisfying. Not every design is successful, but I do feel that the design process is an exercise that is most enjoyable and rewarding.

AN APPROACH TO DESIGN: SHEILA MEYER

Creating my own quilt designs is a fairly new experience for me. Up till recently, I had been more comfortable putting together old patterns in new arrangements, but I never grappled with the idea of designing something entirely new. I arrived at the same plateau that I had come to in weaving. I could produce a well-executed product in a pleasing form. I felt secure as a craftsman but felt that I lacked the genetic endowment or formal training to be an artist, and I felt that one had to be an artist to create new forms and designs.

Then I attended a workshop on design and color given by Michael James, noted quiltmaker and author, and somehow for me it lessened the mystique attached to being an *artist*. I was encouraged to try to make my own designs. Having taken that step, the possibilities seemed endless. One of the first decisions I made was to design a quilt that didn't have to go on a specific bed, fit a certain wall space, or coordinate with the colors of a particular room. Free of these constraints, I could experiment with color and shape and not really concern myself with the destination of the piece. Yet, with no specific use in mind, I was reluctant to commit a great deal of time and fabric to a project. It was then that I started to work on small wall quilts. The following are some of the techniques I now use when working on a new design.

I have many favorites among the traditional designs, and, I have found that, by changing or adding a few lines, totally new shapes emerge. In fig-

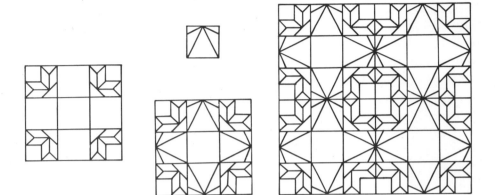

3-7. The traditional *Turkey Tracks* quilt pattern.
3-8. These few lines are added to the plain squares.
3-9. The *Turkey Tracks* pattern now changes dramatically.
3-10. The resulting design.

ure 3-7, *Turkey Tracks* appears in its traditional form. By adding the lines shown in figure 3-8 the blossom or track is continued into the empty squares. The result is the block shown in the figure 3-9. This represents quite a change, given the fact that only a few lines have been added. This design, which is no longer *Turkey Tracks*, can now be made in fabric, either separated by sashing strips (see Glossary) or as shown in figure 3-10.

I keep several sizes of graph paper and several grids on hand when I work on designs. Each grid suggests different potential units and produces quite different results. A large number of the old favorites are based on the nine-patch (figure 3-11). *Shoo-Fly, Ohio Star,* and *Turkey Tracks* are only a few of the familiar ones. In order to preserve the grid for reuse, I place a piece of transparent paper over it. Then I join points and draw lines until I come up with a block that I like. Although the block may be symmetrical, it does not have to be. After many rather unexciting diagrams, I generally find one I like (figure 3-12). I repeat this unit several times on the grid. It may look great with one block next to another facing the same direction (figure 3-13), or it might just be another boring group of lines. I then cut out the individual block units and rearrange them several times. If an interesting design emerges, I fix the blocks in place with a glue stick (figure 3-14).

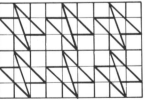
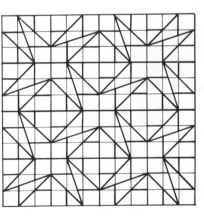

3-11. The nine-patch grid, upon which many traditional favorites are built.

3-12. A new quilt block design.
3-13. When repeated, the new design looks like this.
3-14. The result of rearranging each individual block.

Such old patterns as *Crown and Thorns, Churn Dash,* and *Flying Geese* are based on the five-patch (figure 3-15). While using this or any other grid, I try many compositions of lines until I hit upon one that appeals to me. This may be just the beginning of a design that may require many changes before completion. Let me follow the process by which I arrived at the design for **Amethystine** (see page 127). I worked with the twenty-five-square grid (five-patch) using tracing paper until I arrived at this asymmetrical block (figure 3-16). I wanted to have a central motif that was large enough to occupy the top of a double or queen-size bed. I made the graph squares equal to 4 inches and the block 20 inches. At first, I planned the design as a medallion surrounded by borders (figure 3-17). The four main blocks were to be separated by strips to prevent the sixteen points from converging at the center (something I try to avoid whenever possible).

Before committing myself to this design arrangement, I made copies of the block, cut them out, and rotated them. The results were very exciting. Rather than the more controlled design, the rearrangement produced more contemporary patterns, as shown (figures 3-18 and 3-19). You can see how important it can be to experiment by rotating the blocks rather than holding to a predetermined plan. You may decide that the original design was the best anyway, but try other possibilities first. Consider also that variations of one design could result in several quilts.

Every design you make may not be your magnum opus—it may be good enough to make up in fabric or it may never leave graph paper. It is important to make many designs, as this will increase your chances of meeting with success. I keep all of my graph-paper creations in a folder for future reference. Sometimes when I look back at rejected designs, I find that a small modification can make a big difference. I feel a great sense of satisfaction when I complete a quilt that started out as a thought, an image, or some lines on a sheet of graph paper.

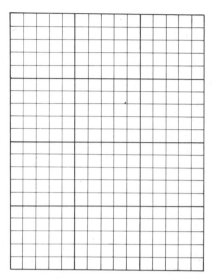
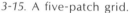

3-15. A five-patch grid.

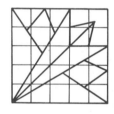

3-16. An asymmetrical block made of the five-patch grid.

3-17. The design created by repeating the new block.

3-18. This design was created as a result of some additional experimentation.

3-19. Still further experimentation. produced this design.

AN APPROACH TO DESIGN: JUDY ROBBINS

When I was in school, one of my teachers told a story about Ernest Hemingway that impressed me greatly. He said that every morning Hemingway would sit down at his typewriter and remain there for four hours. Sometimes he just sat. Sometimes he wrote "garbage." Sometimes he wrote *The Sun Also Rises*. What appealed to me then, as it does now, is Hemingway's attitude. He was able to accept the writer's block and the full wastebaskets that came along with the great American novel. Since I am my own worst critic, I have to remind myself to work along steadily, striving for that Hemingway-like magnanimous acceptance of my own failures as well as successes.

For me, inspiration usually comes during work, not before it. If the muse comes to call on me, it's when I have already made a show of good faith by plunging into a project idea, working and thinking it through.

I am very visually oriented. My ideas come in the form of pictures that I would like to translate into quilts—the rusts and lime greens of the Connecticut River valley in early spring or Ash Swamp in August, dark green grasses, brown cattails, and a nameless violet marsh weed which flowers profusely among the grass. Translating these mental pictures into fabric is a puzzle—a game I play with myself. The puzzle always has many solutions and I only have to find one, though occasionally I will find an idea so intriguing that I work out two or three solutions. I agree to observe a few rules, mainly that the piece will fit the traditional definition of "quilt," having three layers of fabric.

The next step in working out the puzzle is to make a sketch directly on graph paper. This sketch is then simplified to basic geometric forms. The grid on the graph paper makes this easy to do.

Up to this point, all the work has been done in black and white, but it is the translation into color that is the crucial step, one which I approached in a hit-or-miss way for many years. It always bothered me that I did not have a workable, systematic way for experimenting with fabric colors in a quilt. I tried coloring sketches with colored markers. This did not give me a very true picture of what the quilt would look like. I tried making sample pieces. This proved very time consuming. I saw my students struggling with these problems, too.

Out of this frustration grew the technique I call "fabric graphing"—a way of quickly making pasted scale models of quilts. I rarely make a quilt now without fabric graphing it first. My students, too, have received the technique most enthusiastically.

Fabric graphing allows the finished quilt to be seen *before* it is made, before yards of costly material have been purchased, before time and energy have been put on the line. Many people think they need design or art training to make beautiful quilts. My students keep proving over and over that this is not true. We all have a reliable, innate aesthetic sense that we can call upon once we can see what the quilt will look like through the use of fabric graphs. Designing is a continual parade of choices. Fabric graphing takes away the guesswork by showing *exactly* how the various choices will look. Once the scale model, or fabric graph, is made and the design can be clearly seen, then there is only one question to be asked: "Do I like it?" To answer this question, I draw on that same innate aesthetic sense that helps me to select clothes, decorate my home, and pick out what I like in an art museum. I only try to please myself. If I do not like what I see, it is easy to change an 8- by 10-inch pasted model. Colors can be added or removed. Patterns can be adjusted easily.

In this section I have given step-by-step instructions for making fabric graphs. I invite you to get out your fabric scraps and play with the idea. I rarely paste up a whole quilt. A corner section with borders, or the central medallion, will give me a good enough picture to proceed confidently.

Put away your sewing machine, needles and thread, and get out the following:

    your quilt block pattern
    a glue stick
    graph paper
    pencil
    ruler
    small piece of lightweight cardboard
    sharp (very important!) scissors; scissors for paper cutting
    small scraps of selected fabric

Then proceed as follows:

1. Start with a block pattern. For an example we will use *Kaleidoscope* or *World Without End* (figure 3-20). Transfer the block pattern to graph paper, keeping it fairly small. We will use a 1-inch block as an example here (though until you become used to working with small pieces, you may prefer to use a 2- or 3-inch block).

2. If your quilt is to be "set solid," that is, block against block, draw at least four blocks on the graph paper (figure 3-21). You will need that many to get a look at any secondary patterns and to see the way the colors interplay. If your quilt is to be set with sashes, that is, each block set apart by strips of fabric (figure 3-22), draw at least four blocks on the graph paper, set apart to show the sashed area.

3. You are now going to make some tiny templates. Draw the block to measure 1 inch on the graph paper (figure 3-23). Using the glue stick, glue the drawing to the lightweight cardboard. Now, using paper scissors, cut apart the pieces. For the *Kaleidoscope* pattern, you will have three templates, A, B, and C, shown actual size (figure 3-24). If you have nimble fingers, you will be able to work with pieces this size. If you know from experience that you are more agile with larger pieces, simply scale the drawing up to 2 or even 3 inches before cutting it apart to make templates. Two-inch templates are shown (figure 3-25).

4. Next, you will cut the fabric. Use either method described here and do not worry if accuracy suffers. For once in quiltmaking, accuracy is not critical.

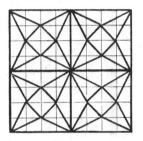

3-20. The *Kaleidoscope* block.

3-21. Four *Kaleidoscope* blocks set solid.

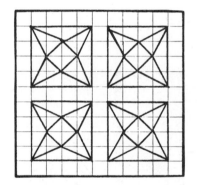

3-22. Four *Kaleidoscope* blocks set with sashes.

49

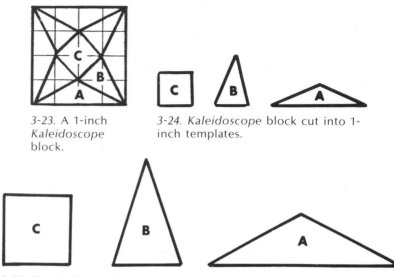

3-23. A 1-inch *Kaleidoscope* block.

3-24. *Kaleidoscope* block cut into 1-inch templates.

3-25. Two-inch templates.

Method 1: Fold the fabric into four layers. Hold the cardboard template under your thumb on top of the layers. Cut around the template with very sharp scissors.

Method 2: Place the template on four layers of cloth. Trace around the template with thin-line felt marker or ballpoint pen. (This is usually a no-no, but it's OK here!) Cut through the four layers on the traced mark. Soon you will have a little pile of tiny pieces on your work surface.

5. The next step is gluing. A glue stick is the very best kind for this purpose. Rub the glue stick over a 1-inch (or larger, if you have scaled up) area on a sheet of graph paper. Using the lines on the graph paper and your drawing of the block as guidelines, place the fabric pieces onto the sticky spot on the graph paper. (If your design is complex, you may want to draw it on the graph paper and place the fabric pieces right over the drawing.) Paste up enough of the quilt so that you will have a good idea of what it will look like.

The *Kaleidoscope* block, in a simple, repeating pattern (I'll call this Plan A) is shown in figure 3-26. Three fabrics were used (black, white, and dotted). Four blocks were pasted. This would be one of the simplest interpretations of *Kaleidoscope*.

3-26. Plan A—the *Kaleidoscope* in a simple repeated pattern.

In looking at the line drawing of four *Kaleidoscope* blocks together, a secondary pattern caught my eye and I decided to emphasize it (figure 3-27). The same three fabrics are used, but this design (Plan B) creates a different effect than Plan A. The difference is one of focus. Plan B focuses on four blocks at a time, while Plan A sees one block at a time.

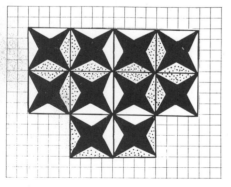

3-27. Plan B—a secondary *Kaleidoscope* pattern.

Because of the way the lines of this pattern converge, there are a number of patterns that emerge. I pasted up ten blocks before I decided that the design in Plan B was clearly revealed.

To experiment some more I penciled sixteen *Kaleidoscope* blocks, set solid in rows of four, on graph paper (Plan C). Looking at the penciled lines, I saw possibilities for this to become a medallion-type design. One more fabric has been added (figure 3-28).

Plan C is more sophisticated than its sisters, but its evolution is apparent. It is no harder to piece than are Plans A or B. The fabrics are essentially the same in all three versions. The difference, again, is focus. In Plan C, the fabric graphs were "played" one step further. Actually, I made several changes in Plan C before I came up with this one, which pleased me. All of the changes, however, took me only twenty minutes of "fooling around," a small investment in time; and, since I was using throwaway-sized scraps, there was no monetary investment. It is very easy to make changes in fabric graphs. Glue stick dries slowly, but you can move pieces around by peeling them off even after the glue has dried completely. Fabric graphing offers the quiltmaker unparalleled freedom to experiment.

There are some quilts for which this technique is not suitable. These include appliqué quilts and pieced patterns with many small pieces, such as *Feathered Star* or *Delectable Mountains*. It should be noted, however, that tiny pieces, such as those that occur in *Feathered Star*, "read" as solid colors even if they are prints. Here is one case where felt markers are useful. You will notice, too, that large prints become lost in small-scale models. When using a large print, the model will be less visually accurate, but still significantly better than markers.

You will find many applications for fabric graphs. Quiltmakers who work by commission will find that a model made of actual fabric samples is often easier for a client to "see" than a sketch. Students and teachers find this a good way to explore color theory. My students routinely make fabric graphs as part of quilt planning. The small amount of time spent in making fabric graphs is well spent because it allows you to proceed confidently, knowing that your fabric choices are sound and that your quilt will look just as you had envisioned.

3-28. Plan C—a more sophisticated *Kaleidoscope* pattern.

AN APPROACH TO DESIGN: MICKEY LAWLER

My work stems from two distinctly different sources: inspiration, which is free, unlimited pleasure; and perseverance, a determination I call on only when I must work within certain limits (deadlines, for instance, or specific colors and fabrics).

The inspired moments make designing a new quilt easy and exciting. Ideas for patterns come quickly and seem to be self-perpetuating. A building, new fabric, the shadow of some wind chimes, even the pattern on my kitchen floor or the pattern of the panes of glass in the antique window of my shop can inspire me to graph geometric shapes far into the night. As a graph-paper addict, I draw and redraw countless lines, then color and recolor until I have a stack of possibilities. Next, I leave all this in a pile on my chaotic desk for a day or so. When I go back to my drawings, many are dismissed into folders for future use, but I usually find one design, color and all, that demands attention.

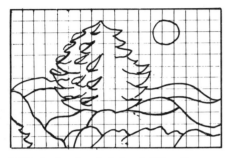

3-29. A simple sketch of **After the Storm** on graph paper.

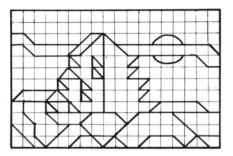

3-30. The design adapted to the grid network.

As much as I admire people who randomly cut fabric until they find the right design, I still like the security of a specific graph-paper plan before cutting into any of my material. Furthermore, I long ago gave up trying to find fabric that duplicates my colored pencils. It's just too futile and time consuming! I approximate the graph-paper colors or sometimes change the colors altogether. Deciding which is the most important area of the design, I begin by choosing the fabric for that, and bring others into place around it. I stack up bolts of cloth and stand at least 10 feet back. Squinting at the bolts from this distance blends the fabrics much the same way they will be in a quilt. I then restack more bolts and repeat the procedure. By this time I can usually tell whether one fabric is too dominant or not dominant enough, whether the colors blend or contrast as they should for that particular design.

One winter, as Judy, Sarah, Sheila, and I got together, the title **After The Storm** (see page 55) was tossed about as inspiration for a wall quilt. Later, I noticed the pine trees near our house had gathered great white mounds of snow on their branches. By roughly sketching the scene on graph paper (figure 3-29). I found that the grids naturally broke the design into squares and triangles. This type of piece is fun and quite simple since it is really a graph-paper mosaic (figure 3-30). I then decided that nighttime colors would be far easier to find and much more dramatic than Connecticut's gray winter day colors. The first fabric I chose was for the sky. A crisp print—clear white specks on a dark navy background—was perfect. The specks looked like stars in the night sky. From that followed the darkest greens I could find for the tree and white and pale blues for the snow and the moon. Somehow the plain white moon seemed too trite, too unrealistic. I waited for night to come and went outside. The sky was streaked with dark clouds, which occasionally passed across the moon. I added a navy streak across the moon and sky in my drawing and to my growing stack of fabrics and was, at last, pleased with the result.

I always give my selection of fabrics a final test by holding the combination up to a mirror. This little trick never fails to provide a fresh, objective look at the total effect. Choosing the right fabrics usually takes at least as much time as the designing process, but, at the end of all this, I can go on with confidence to the enjoyment of cutting and sewing.

Inspiration for new designs, however, does not always come just when I may need some drawings to submit for a client's consideration or for a new quilt for an impending show. These are the times when I know I must persevere. I make myself block out a few 1- or 2-inch squares on graph paper and then begin dividing them with lines. Just three or four lines at strange angles are often interesting enough to create enthusiasm for the new project. It is very important to keep that first square quite simple. The temptation is often to draw something complex, but, when a complex square is multiplied, the design can become an unruly maze of lines. Next I draw a duplicate square beside the first to see what will happen if I make a straight series. If that looks promising, I simply keep going; if not, I begin turning the original square.

End of the Tracks (see page 58) is an example of a relatively simple square (figure 3-31) repeated and quarter-turned three times (figure 3-32). (The same square in a straight series would have resulted in a totally different look, as shown in figure 3-33). What began as an assymetrical square ends in a harmonious, graphic block. A series of these larger blocks forms an interesting bed-size quilt.

3-31. **The End of the Tracks** block.

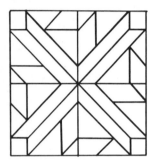

3-32. **The End of the Tracks** block repeated four times, each time turned a quarter-turn.

3-33. **The End of the Tracks** block repeated three times in a series.

If you arrive at a design that excites you, try out a range of different color combinations. **After the Storm** might be great as *Summer Sunset*. Instead of tediously duplicating the line drawings, I often graph my latest favorite with black marker and make a few photocopies. Then all I have left is the pure pleasure of coloring it in, and pleasure in the creation is, after all, the real result I seek in all the lines and squares and graph paper.

4

Twenty Contemporary Quilts

The twenty quilts that follow represent a variety of styles, moods, and themes. Some are more "contemporary" than others; some are traditional in terms of their design, but contemporary in terms of their use of color.

For each of the twenty projects we've presented thorough instructions. The Materials and Cutting Chart tells you how many different colors of fabric are needed (a color code number is assigned to each fabric), the yardage necessary, and how many Pattern Pieces are to be cut from each fabric.

Pattern Pieces are provided, full size, for each part. Simply trace them directly from the book. Be sure to add the ¼-inch seam allowance unless otherwise noted. The Color Placement Guide, which is a complete drawing of the finished quilt, is coded with the numbers listed on the Materials·and Cutting Chart. To assemble each quilt block, simply follow this guide, the Piecing Together drawings, and the written instructions.

Remember that the colors listed in the chart are the colors we used, and certainly not the only choices available to you. Experiment on your own to come up with your own combinations. It might be a good idea to review Chapter 3 to understand better the relationship between color and the overall impact of the quilt design.

Remember too that you can change the size of the quilt by adding borders or panels of extra quilt blocks.

AFTER THE STORM

After the Storm is a geometric picture quilt based on a mosaic technique. Squares and triangles of different colors are joined together to represent a snow-laden tree silhouetted against a starry sky.

Straight seam lines make this an extremely easy design to piece, and it's fun to watch the picture grow as you sew!

4-1. **After the Storm.** Designed by Mickey Lawler.

MATERIALS AND CUTTING CHART

Fabrics	Yardage	Cutting Instructions
1. dark print	¾ yard	88A, 13B
2. navy	¼ yard	11A, 6B
3. white	⅜ yard	15A, 35B, 1C, 1D
4. dark green	⅞ yard	12A, 20B
		Borders: 2 strips 2½ by 24½ inches, 2 strips 2½ by 40½ inches (seams included on border)
5. medium green	⅓ yard	18A, 13B
6. medium blue	⅛ yard	5A, 4B
7. light blue	⅛ yard	14A, 11B
8. Backing	⅞ yard	

¼-inch seam allowances are not included unless indicated.

FINISHED SIZE: 28 BY 40 INCHES

PIECING INSTRUCTIONS

1. Using the Pattern Pieces provided, trace and cut pieces according to Cutting Instructions. Add ¼-inch seam allowances before cutting.

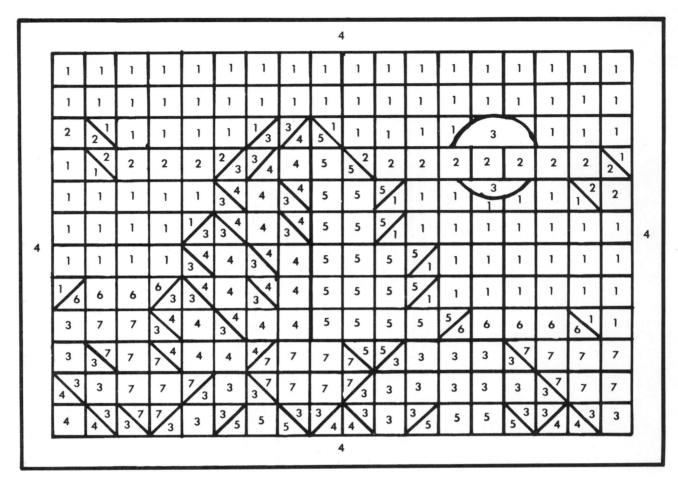

4-2. Color Placement Guide.

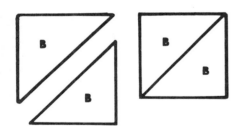

4-3. Piecing together.

2. Using the Color Placement Guide, sew all triangles (Pattern Piece B) together to form squares (figure 4-3), matching colors according to the Color Placement Guide.

3. Next sew all the squares (Pattern Piece A as well as the squares formed by sewing together the Pattern Piece B triangles) together in horizontal rows, starting from the top of the Color Placement Guide. For example, the top row and the second row from the top are each simply 18 dark print squares.

4. Next, sew the top row to the second row from the top, matching seams carefully.

5. Continue sewing squares to form horizontal rows.

Note: The moon (Pattern Pieces C and D) is blindstitched in place after the whole top has been pieced. The squares that are covered by the moon are dark print.

6. Continue sewing each row to the next, referring to the Color Placement Guide to make sure all pieces are placed correctly. There are twelve horizontal rows in all.

7. Once the rows are all sewn together, blindstitch the moon (Pattern Pieces C and D) in place.

8. Next sew the 2½- by 24½-inch border strips to each side of the piece. Then sew the 2½- by 40½-inch border strips to the top and bottom.

Add ¼-inch seam allowances to all Pattern Pieces.

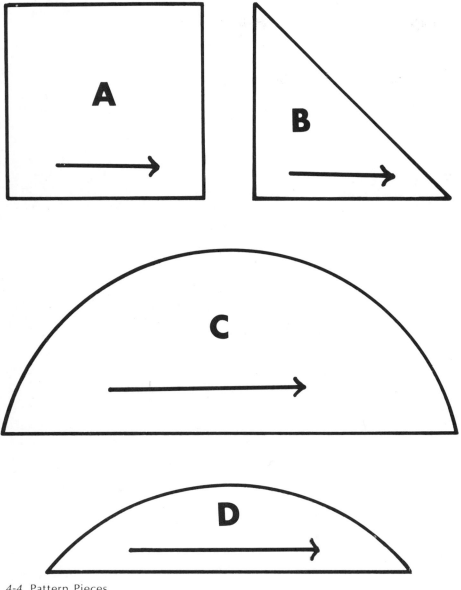

4-4. Pattern Pieces.

QUILTING

Very little of this design must be marked for quilting. Most of the shapes are outline quilted. However, there are diagonal quilting lines in the medium green portion of the tree. These should be drawn onto the fabric about 1½ inches apart. Layer, baste, and quilt.

FINISHING

Bind the edges of the quilt with a separate straight binding (see page 27).

END OF THE TRACKS

Reminiscent of the stacks of railroad ties at the end of the tracks, this bold design takes on a three-dimensional quality by the use of three shades of color against a solid background (figure 4-5). Architectural in appearance, it is, nevertheless, an easy design to piece.

4-5. **End of the Tracks.** Designed by Mickey Lawler.

MATERIALS AND CUTTING CHART

Fabrics	Yardage	Cutting Instructions
1. white	1 ¾ yards	4A, 4C
		Borders: 4 strips 3 by 30 inches; 31-inch square for backing
2. light brown	⅓ yard	4D, 4E, 4G
3. medium brown	⅓ yard	4A, 4Br
4. dark brown	⅓ yard	4B, 4F

"r" indicates the reverse side of the pattern.
¼-inch seam allowances are not included.

FINISHED SIZE: 30 BY 30 INCHES

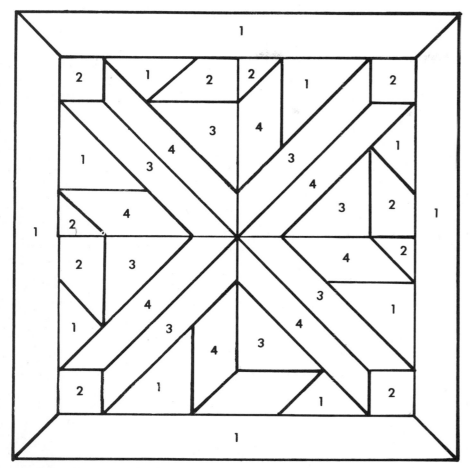

4-6. Color Placement Guide.

PIECING INSTRUCTIONS

1. Using the Pattern Pieces provided, trace and cut pieces according to the Cutting Instructions. Add ¼-inch seam allowances before cutting.

2. Each of the four blocks in this design is identical. Follow the illustrations to piece together. To form the first block, sew E to F. Then sew a white A to F (figure 4-8). This forms a large triangle.

3. Sew C to G. Then sew a medium brown A to G (figure 4-9). This forms another large triangle.

4. Sew B to Br and set D into this unit (figure 4-10).

5. Finally sew the two A units to the B unit (using figure 4-7 as a guide). The first block is now complete.

6. Construct three more of the blocks and sew them together to form the design shown in the Color Placement Guide.

7. Finally sew on the white borders, mitering the corners (see page 29).

QUILTING

Mark quilting lines in straight rows about 1 inch apart, following the photograph. Layer the top, batting, and backing. Baste the layers together and hand quilt.

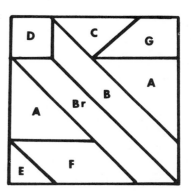

4-7. Twelve-inch Quilt Block.

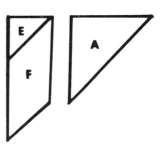

4-8. Piecing together A, E, and F.

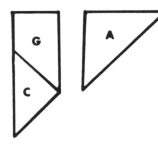

4-9. Piecing together A, G, and C.

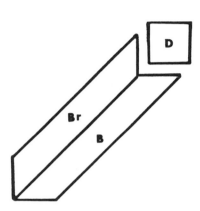

4-10. Piecing together Br, B, and D.

FINISHING

Bind the edges of the quilt with a separate straight binding (see page 27).

VARIATION

Six of these designs would make a beautiful single-bed quilt measuring 54 by 78 inches. One or two borders might be added to make the quilt larger (figure 4-11).

4-11. A variation of the **End of the Tracks** pattern.

Add ¼-inch seam allowances to all Pattern Pieces.

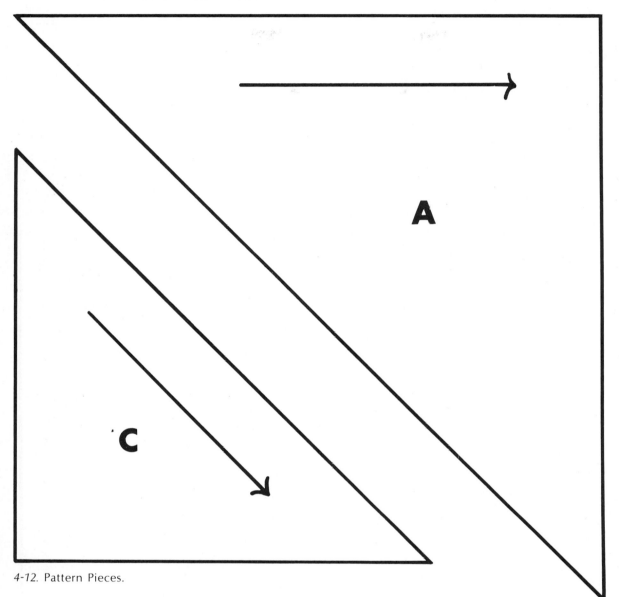

4-12. Pattern Pieces.

Tape pieces together at dotted lines to form Pattern Piece B.
Add ¼-inch seam allowance at solid lines.

B

B

4-12. Pattern Pieces.

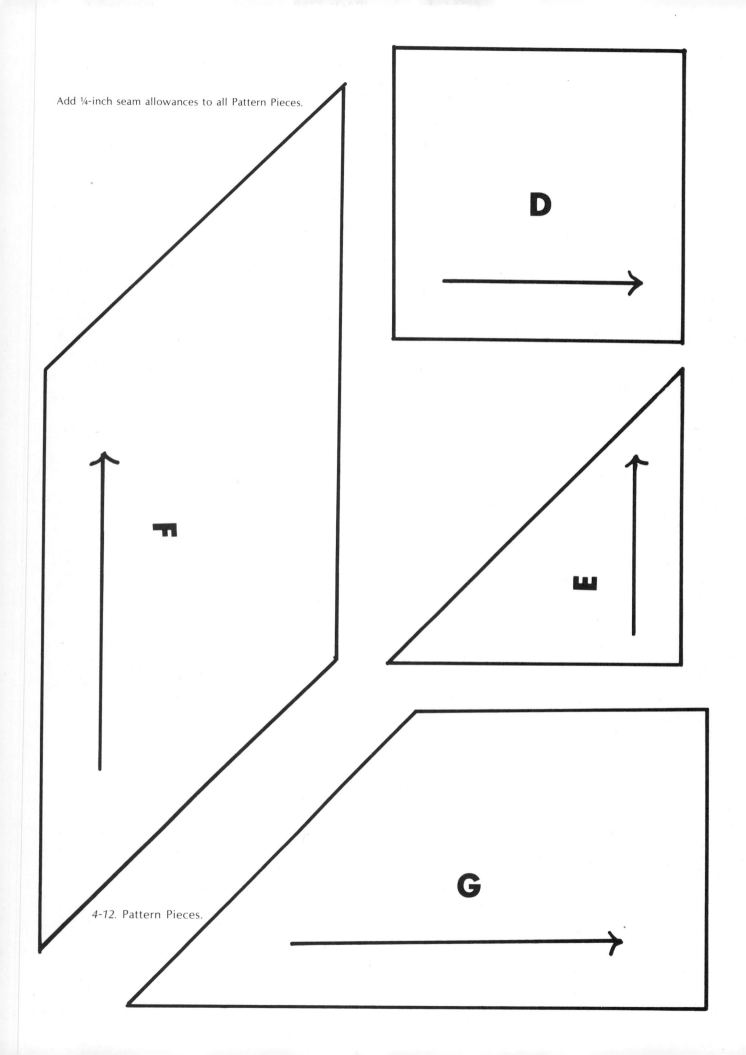

Add ¼-inch seam allowances to all Pattern Pieces.

D

F

E

4-12. Pattern Pieces.

G

DANIEL

Although the basis for this design is the organized and logical piecing of a typical traditional quilt, the color arrangement provides an intricate pattern and totally overshadows the static block from which it is derived. The light tones become deeper as they progress toward the edges, creating a sense of warmth and illuminating the center of the design.

4-13. **Daniel**. Designed by Mickey Lawler.

MATERIALS AND CUTTING CHART

Fabrics	Yardage	Cutting Instructions
1. rust red	1 ⅓ yards	72A, 36B, 72C Binding: Cut 4 strips 1½ inch wide the full length of the fabric.
2. off-white	½ yard	8A, 8B, 16C, 1D
3. peach	½ yard	8A, 8B, 20C, 4D
4. melon	½ yard	18A, 20B, 36C, 4D
5. Backing	1 ⅓ yards	

¼-inch seam allowances are not included.

FINISHED SIZE: 45 BY 45 INCHES

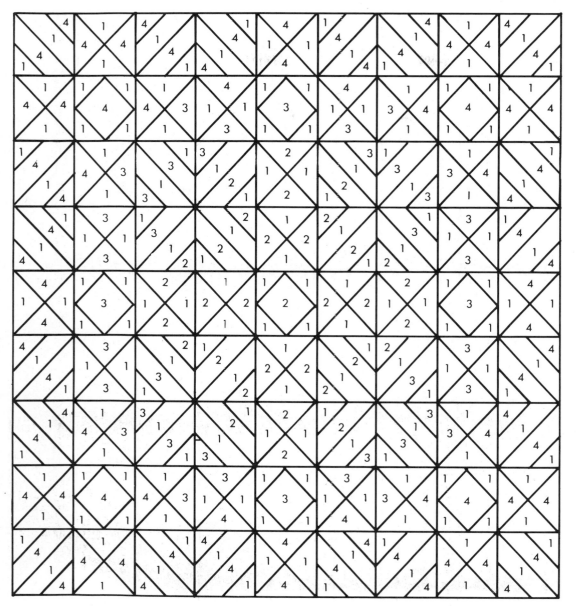

4-14. Color Placement Guide.

PIECING INSTRUCTIONS

1. Using the Pattern Pieces provided, trace and cut pieces according to the Cutting Instructions. Add ¼-inch seam allowances before cutting.

2. Follow the Color Placement Guide, the Quilt Block drawing, and the illustrations that follow to assemble each block. Sew A to B (figure 4-16). Repeat. Then sew the two AB sections together to form a square (figure 4-17). Although the color combinations may vary, there will be four of these squares in each block.

3. Sew an A to each side of a D (figure 4-18) to form a square. There is only one of these squares in the center of each block.

4. Sew two Cs together (figure 4-19). Repeat. Then sew the two C sections

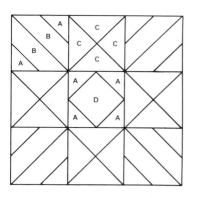

4-15. Fifteen-inch Quilt Block.

65

together to form a square (figure 4-20). Again, the color combinations may vary, but there will always be four of these squares in each block.

5. Sew these nine completed squares together to form the block (figure 4-15).

6. There are nine blocks in the quilt (three rows of three blocks each). Join the nine blocks together, paying careful attention to the Color Placement Guide.

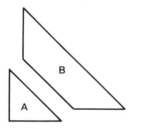

4-16. Piecing together A and B.

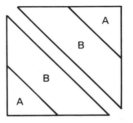

4-17. Piecing together AB and AB.

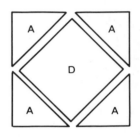

4-18. Piecing together four As and D.

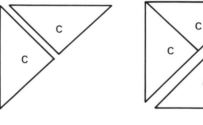

4-19. Piecing together Cs.

4-20. Piecing together four Cs to make a square.

QUILTING

Daniel is outline quilted ⅛ inch inside the seam line of each of the off-white, peach, and melon pieces. There is no quilting in any of the rust red shapes.

FINISHING

A separate straight binding is sewn to the front of the piece, folded over the back, and hand stitched in place. A sleeve is attached to the top back to accommodate a firring strip for hanging the quilt.

VARIATIONS

To make this quilt larger, you may draft your own pattern pieces on a larger scale or simply add more blocks. Adding one more row of blocks on all four sides would make this a beautiful bed quilt.

Add ¼-inch seam allowances to all Pattern Pieces.

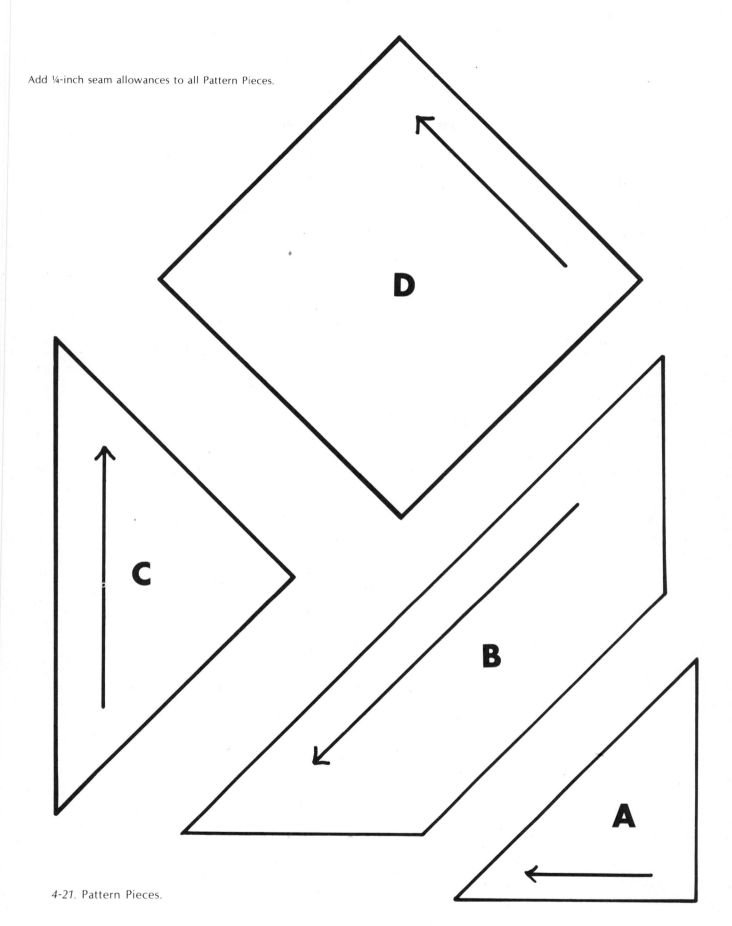

4-21. Pattern Pieces.

GULF SUNRISE

Soft warm and cool colors portray earth, sea, and sky in harmony within the vastness of space. Inspired by the beauty of Florida's Gulf coast, this design is fun to construct because the quilter moves quickly from one technique to the next.

MATERIALS AND CUTTING CHART

Fabrics	Yardage	Cutting Instructions
1. navy	⅞ yard	one 30½-inch square
2. dusty melon	½ yard	1A
3. willow green	¼ yard	2 strips 1½ by 21 inches Borders: 2 strips 1½ by 34½ inches, 2 strips 1½ by 36½ inches.
4. gray	⅛ yard	2 strips 1½ by 21 inches
5. dusty blue	⅛ yard	2 strips 1½ by 21 inches
6. rose	⅛ yard	2 strips 1½ by 21 inches
7. peach	¼ yard	2 strips 1½ by 21 inches Borders: 2 strips 1½ by 30½ inches, 2 strips 1½ by 32½ inches.
8. mauve	¼ yard	2 strips 1½ by 21 inches Borders: 2 strips 1½ by 32½ inches, 2 strips 1½ by 34½ inches.
9. pale blue	⅛ yard	2 strips 1½ by 21 inches
10. pale pink	1 ⅛ yard	2 strips 1½ by 21 inches 36½-inch square for backing

Add ¼-inch seam allowance to Pattern Piece A before cutting.
All other pieces *include* ¼-inch seam allowances.

FINISHED SIZE: 36 BY 36 INCHES

PIECING INSTRUCTIONS

1. To draft Pattern Piece A, draw a circle 20 inches in diameter on a large piece of brown paper. A compass made from string and a piece of chalk works well. The string should be 10 inches long to draw a circle with a 20-inch diameter. Mark the center of the circle. Place a yardstick across the center point and draw a line across the circle. Then mark two secondary points on this line 5 inches from the center. (These points will also be 5 inches from either side of the circle). Next draw two new circles, each 10 inches in diameter, using the secondary points as centers (figure 4-24). The top half of one circle and the bottom half of the other will form Pattern Piece A. All other pieces for **Gulf Sunrise** are included in the Materials and Cutting Chart.

2. Add ¼-inch seam allowance to Pattern Piece A and cut it out. All other pieces *include* ¼-inch seam allowances.

3. Arrange 16 strips 1½ by 21 inches in a progression from warm to cool colors. Sew the strips together lengthwise, taking ¼-inch seams, until you have a rectangle 16½ inches wide by 21 inches long.

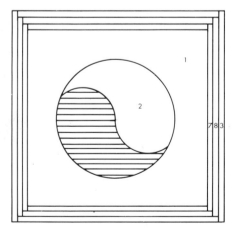

4-23. Color Placement Guide.

4-22. **Gulf Sunrise.** Designed by Mickey Lawler.

4. Cut one Pattern Piece A from this rectangle of strips (figure 4-25) and one Pattern Piece A from dusty melon.

5. Blindstitch the dusty melon A to the stripped A along seam line to form a circle.

6. Blindstitch circle in the center of the navy 30½-inch-square.

7. From the back, carefully trim away navy fabric ¼ inch inside the edges of the circle to prevent the navy from showing through the light-colored strips.

BORDERS

1. Sew 1½- by 30½-inch strips of peach to top and bottom of navy square. Then sew 1½- by 32½-inch strips to each side.

2. Add 1½- by 32½-inch strips of mauve to top and bottom. Sew 1½- by 34½-inch strips to each side.

3. Finally add 1½- by 34½-inch strips of willow green to top and bottom. Sew 1½- by 36½-inch strips to each side. You now have three narrow borders around the navy square.

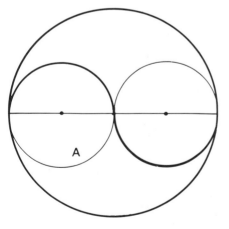

4-24. Drafting Pattern Piece A.

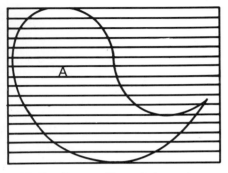

4-25. Cut Pattern Piece A from the striped rectangle.

QUILTING

The quilting design in this piece is also drawn with a string compass. Ever increasing concentric circles in the navy background give motion to the design, and wave or plumelike shapes in a solid half of the circle echo the curves. Straight lines of quilting along the edges of the strips provide a nice contrast.

FINISHING

The edges of **Gulf Sunrise** are hand stitched together, although you may wish to attach an invisible binding (see page 29). A sleeve is sewn to the top of the back to accommodate a firring strip.

VARIATIONS

Using the string compass, you can easily make the design large enough for the center of a bed quilt—a striking focal point for any room.

EASTER

Exploding through the color spectrum, **Easter** heralds the joyful season that inspired its creation.

Because of the great variety of colors and shades in this design, it is important to make a colored diagram to follow when you are piecing. Despite its seemingly complex nature, the piecing of this design is quite simple. There are only three different design blocks.

4-26. **Easter.** Designed by Mickey Lawler.

MATERIALS AND CUTTING CHART

Fabrics	Yardage	Cutting Instructions
1. dark green	⅓ yard	2B, 2Br
2. dark purple	⅓ yard	2B, 2Br
3. dark navy	¾ yard	4A, 4C, 1E, 1Er, 2F
4. bright navy	¾ yard	2A, 1E, 1Er, 2F
5. royal blue	⅓ yard	6A, 2C, 2D, 4F
6. bright blue	⅓ yard	4A, 4C, 2D
7. bright purple	½ yard	2A, 4B, 4Br, 3E, 3Er
8. pale blue	⅓ yard	10A, 4C, 2D
9. bright green	⅓ yard	2B, 2Br
10. lime green	⅓ yard	2B, 2Br
11. pale lavender	¾ yard	4A, 2C, 2E, 2Er
12. rose	⅓ yard	2B, 2Br
13. pale pink	⅓ yard	2B, 2Br, 2C
14. peach	½ yard	6A, 4D
15. melon	¾ yard	8A, 4C, 1E, 1Er, 2F
16. magenta	⅓ yard	2B, 2Br
17. hot pink	¾ yard	2A, 4B, 4Br, 3E, 3Er
18. orange	⅞ yard	4A, 2C, 2D, 4F
19. red	¾ yard	4A, 4C, 1E, 1Er, 2F
20. light yellow	⅓ yard	2B, 2Br
21. bright yellow	⅓ yard	2B, 2Br
22. yellow gold	⅓ yard	2B, 2Br
23. unbleached muslin	4 yards	for backing

"r" indicates the reverse side of the pattern.
¼-inch seam allowances are not included.

FINISHED SIZE: 60 BY 80 INCHES

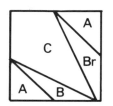

4-28. Quilt Block

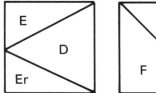

4-29. Quilt Block

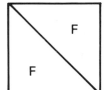

4-30. Quilt Block

PIECING INSTRUCTIONS

1. Using the Pattern Pieces provided, trace and cut pieces according to the Cutting Instructions. Add ¼-inch seam allowances before cutting.
2. The design incorporates three design blocks (figures 4-28 through 4-30), but the color variations are many. Follow the Color Placement Guide carefully as you piece together. For the first block piece A to B and another A to Br (figures 4-31 and 4-32). Then join C to the ABr section (figure 4-33) and finally add the AB section to finish the block (figure 4-34).
3. To form the next block, join D to E (figure 4-35) and add Er (figure 4-36).
4. For the last block join the two F triangles (figures 4-37 and 4-38).
5. Following the Color Placement Guide, join six blocks across. Pay careful attention to the direction of the design and the color placement as you sew each block to the next. Make eight horizontal rows of six blocks each. Then join all the rows together to complete the quilt top.

4-27. Color Placement Guide.

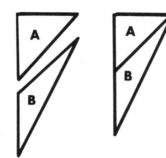
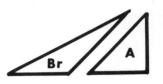
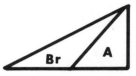

4-31. Piecing together A and B.

4-32. Piecing together A and Br.

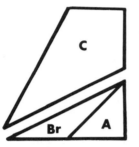
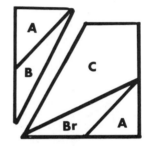
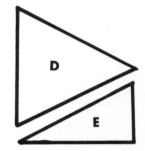

4-33. Piecing together C and ABr.

4-34. Piecing together AB and CABr.

4-35. Piecing together D and E.

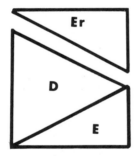
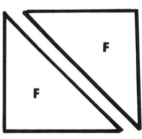
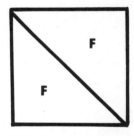

4-36. Piecing together Er and DE.

4-37. Piecing together two Fs.

4-38. Two Fs joined.

QUILTING

Leave the B and Br pieces unquilted. Quilt the remainder of the quilt in lines running from the center of the quilt to the outside edges.

FINISHING

Easter is finished using the invisible binding method (see page 29).

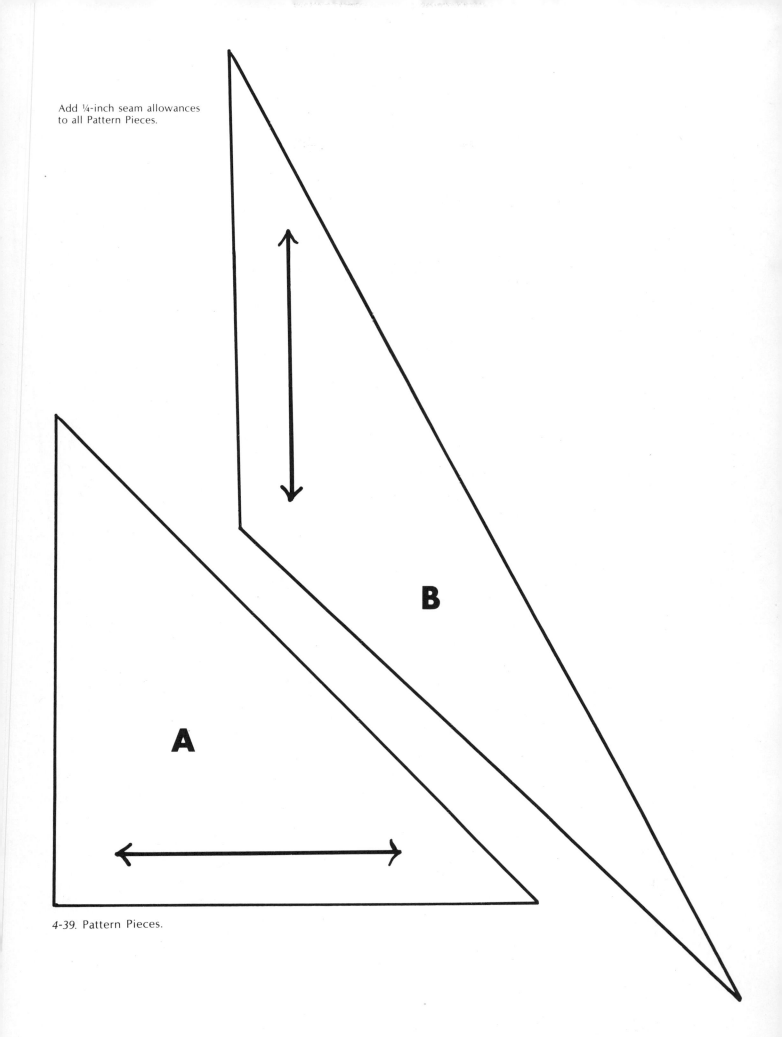

Add ¼-inch seam allowances to all Pattern Pieces.

B

A

4-39. Pattern Pieces.

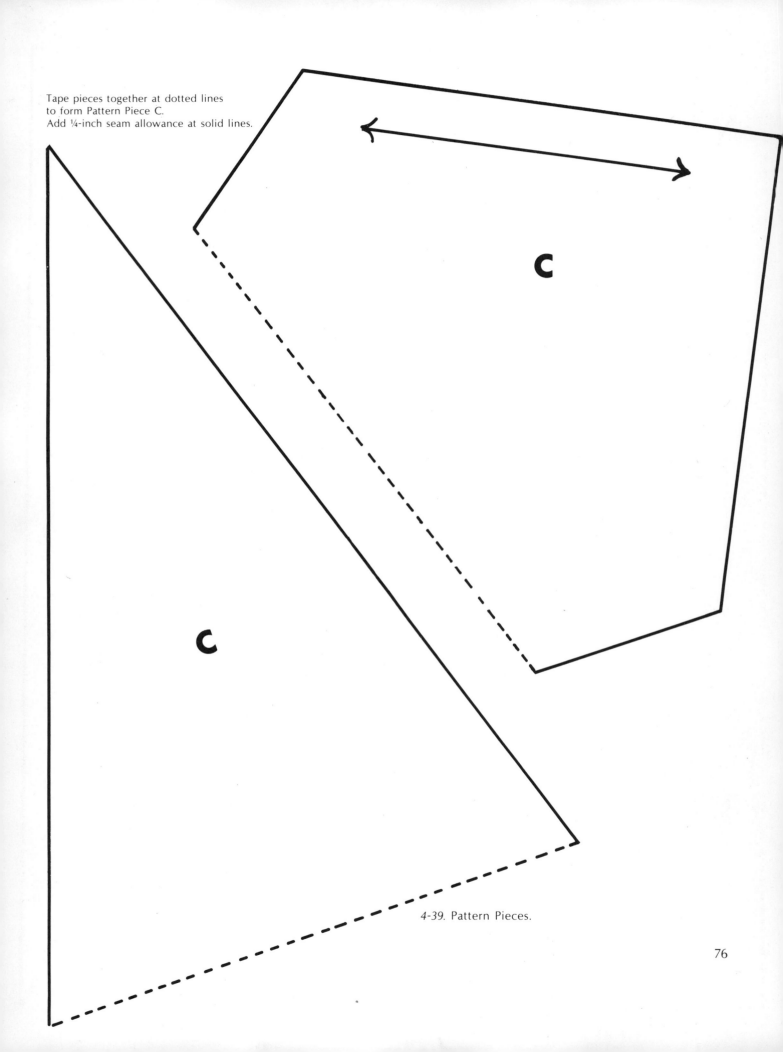

Tape pieces together at dotted lines
to form Pattern Piece C.
Add ¼-inch seam allowance at solid lines.

C

C

4-39. Pattern Pieces.

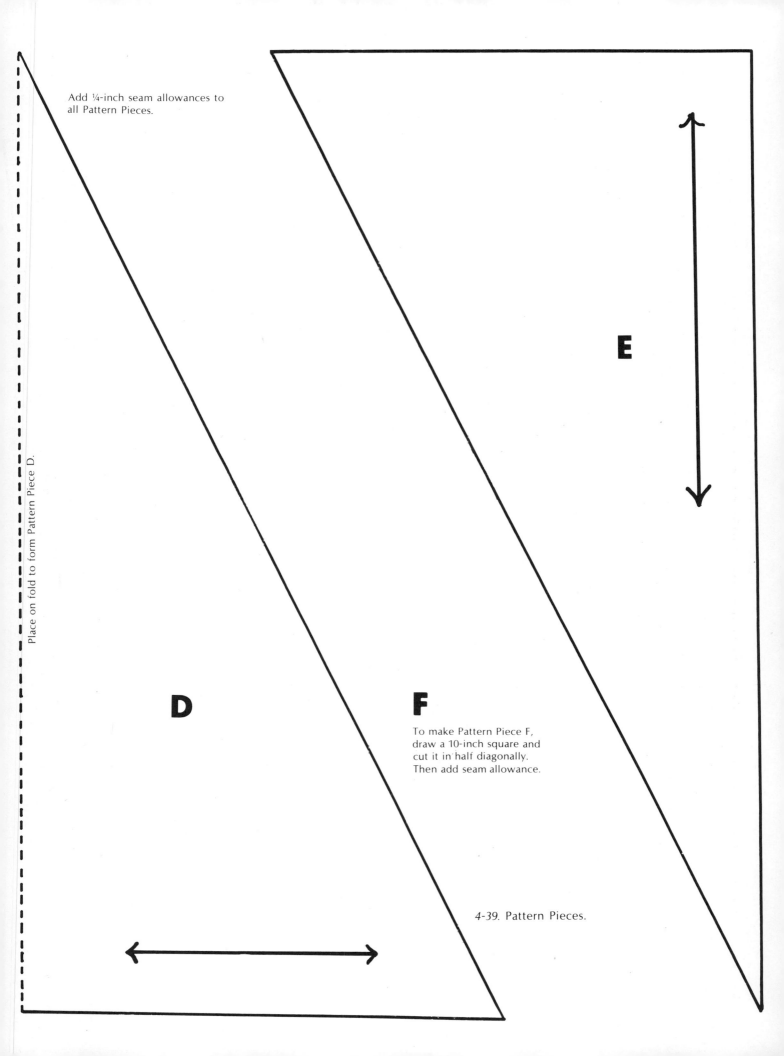

Add ¼-inch seam allowances to all Pattern Pieces.

Place on fold to form Pattern Piece D.

E

D

F

To make Pattern Piece F, draw a 10-inch square and cut it in half diagonally. Then add seam allowance.

4-39. Pattern Pieces.

MEDICINE MAN

The inspiration for **Medicine Man** came from a postcard depicting an Indian wearing ceremonial attire and feathered headdress. In the postcard he is standing on the cliffs of Martha's Vineyard, Massachusetts, overlooking the Atlantic Ocean. The deep teal blue of the ocean and the warm tan of the rocks and sand provide a perfect background for the Indian's colorful costume: his tan leather outfit is trimmed and accented with triangles of red, brown, and turquoise.

Medicine Man consists of four identical 12-inch blocks that form the design for the wall hanging. One border consisting of three narrow strips of colors and one wide, quilted border frame the piece, which is hung with fabric loops and wooden dowels.

MATERIALS AND CUTTING CHART

Fabrics	Yardage	Cutting Instructions*
1. red	⅜ yard	16C 4 border strips: 2 strips 1 by 24½ inches, 2 strips 1 by 25 inches (seams included on borders)
2. teal	⅜ yard	8A, 8Ar 4 border strips: 2 strips 1 by 25½ inches, 2 strips 1 by 26 inches (seams included on borders)
3. brown	⅜ yard	16C 4 border strips: 2 strips 1 by 26½ inches, 2 strips 1 by 27 inches (seams included on borders)
4. white	¼ yard	16B, 8D, 8Dr
5. tan	1¾ yards	8A, 8Ar, 8Dr 4 border strips: 2 strips 4 by 27½ inches, 2 strips 4 by 34 inches (seams included on borders) 4 binding strips: 2 strips 34½ by 1½ inches, 2 strips 35½ by 1½ inches (seams included on binding) 8 pieces 3½ by 6 inches for fabric loops
6. Backing	1 yard	

two wooden dowels 36 inches long and ¾ inch in diameter
"r" indicates reverse side of the pattern
¼-inch seam allowances are not included unless indicated.

*Note: Cut strips for borders and binding across the grain of fabric before cutting pattern pieces.

FINISHED SIZE: 34 BY 34 INCHES

PIECING INSTRUCTIONS

1. Using the Pattern Pieces provided, trace and cut pieces according to the Cutting Instructions. Add ¼ inch for seam allowances before cutting.
2. The design consists of four identical quilt blocks (figure 4-42). We rec-

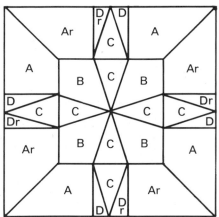

4-42. Twelve-inch Quilt Block.

4-40. **Medicine Man.** Designed by Sarah Doolan Gobes.

ommend hand piecing for this wall hanging because of the slender points and small size of the C and D pieces. The corners of the center white square must be set in, and that, too, is more easily done by hand. To begin, join a white D and Dr piece to each of two red C pieces. Repeat for two brown C and tan D and Dr pieces (figure 4-43).

3. Join a teal A and Ar piece to either side of both brown DCDr units (figure 4-44). You now have two red, white, and tan ADCDrAr units and two brown, tan, and teal ADCDrAr units.

4. For the center square join white B to red C(1) to brown C(3) to white B. Repeat for the other half of the square and join the two (figure 4-45).

5. Join the four ADCDrAr units to each side of the center square, following the Color Placement Guide.

6. Repeat for the remaining three blocks and then sew the four blocks together. Refer to the color photograph for placement of the blocks.

7. Attach the first two red border strips to the top and bottom of the piece, the second two red strips to the sides. The measurements for the borders include the seam allowances so that they may be stitched by machine. Repeat for the teal, brown, and tan borders, always attaching the top and bottom pieces first, and then the sides.

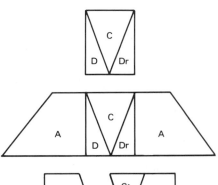

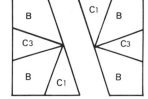

4-43. Piecing together D, C, and Dr.
4-44. Piecing together A, Ar, and DCDr.
4-45. Piecing together the center square.

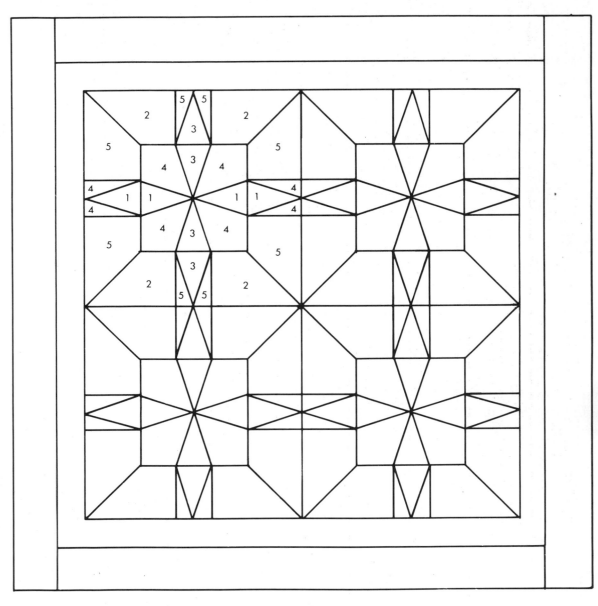

4-41. Color Placement Guide.

QUILTING

Medicine Man is hand quilted, outline quilted ⅜ inch inside the seams of the A and Ar trapezoids. The pattern for the decorative border quilting is provided with the Pattern Pieces.

FINISHING

Finish the hanging with a ½-inch binding (1½-inch cut), and 1½-inch-wide fabric loops (3½-inch cut), four each, evenly spaced, on the top and bottom of the piece. See page 27 for instructions on binding and page 36 on how to make and attach the fabric loops for hanging. Stain two 36-inch-long dowels and insert them through the fabric loops for hanging.

Sunlight Through the Trees.
Designed by Judy Robbins.

Interstices. Designed by Sarah Doolan Gobes.

Optric. Designed by Judy Robbins.

Easter. Designed by Mickey Lawler.

Spring Flower. Designed by Sheila Meyer.

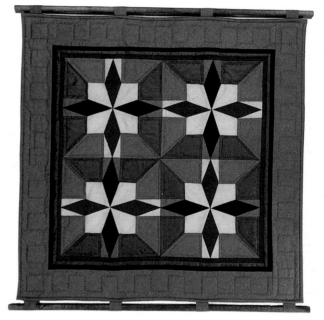

Medicine Man. Designed by Sarah Doolan Gobes.

Interlocking Stars. Designed by Sheila Meyer.

In the Pink. Designed by Judy Robbins.

Amethystine. Designed by Sheila Meyer.

Gulf Sunrise. Designed by Mickey Lawler.

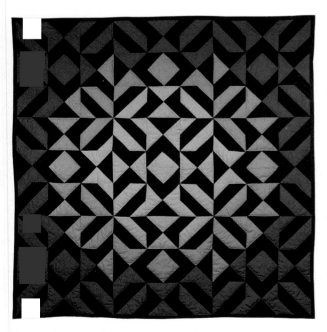

Daniel. Designed by Mickey Lawler.

Peace Dance. Designed by Judy Robbins.

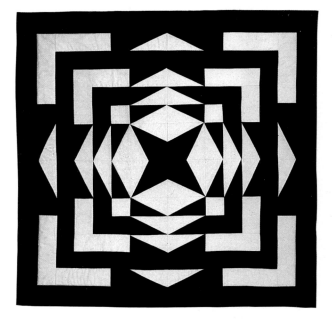

Echo. Designed by Sheila Meyer.

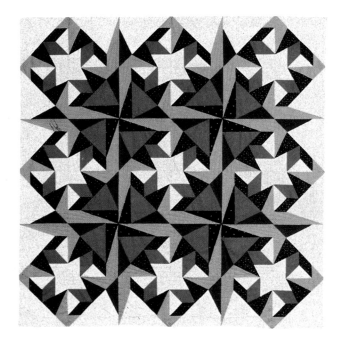

Perpetual Motion. Designed by Sheila Meyer.

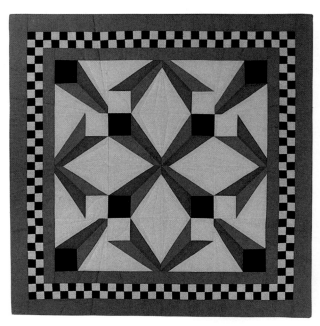

Skyscrapers. Designed by Sarah Doolan Gobes.

River Run. Designed by Judy Robbins.

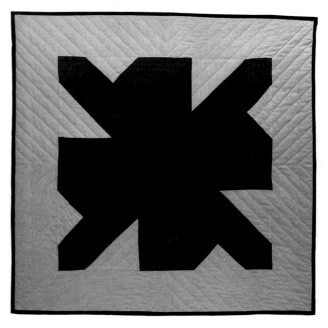

End of the Tracks. Designed by Mickey Lawler.

Birds of a Feather. Designed by Sarah Doolan Gobes.

After the Storm. Designed by Mickey Lawler.

Seminole Star. Designed by Sarah Doolan Gobes.

Add ¼-inch seam allowances to all Pattern Pieces.

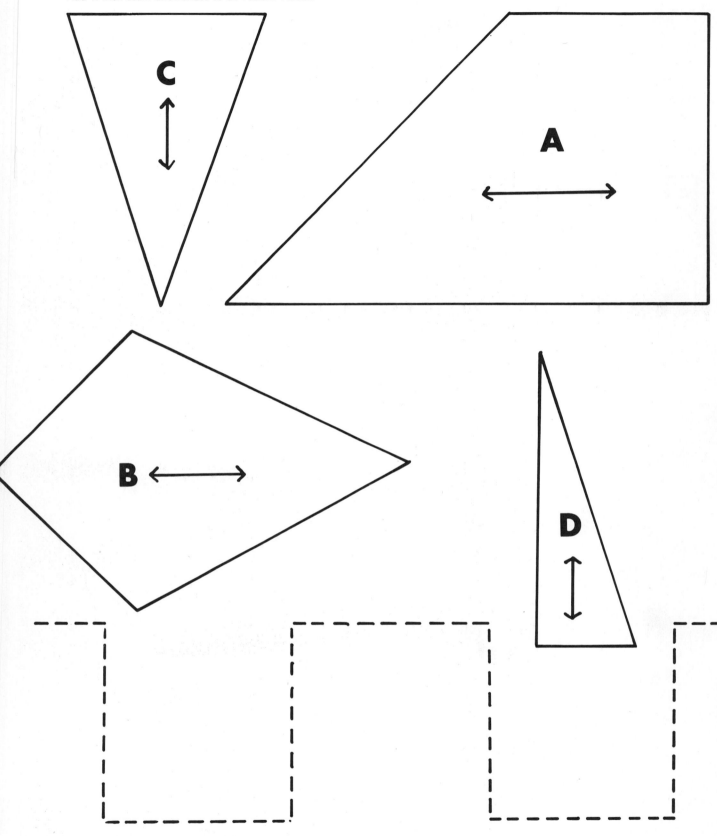

4-46. Pattern Pieces.

BIRDS OF A FEATHER

Birds of a Feather was designed to be a wall hanging composed of four identical 12-inch blocks arranged so that the heads of the "birds" point inward. The resulting central motif, in this quilt a green print, thus becomes the focal point because of its strong color. Using a light color for pieces E and G makes the design recede, and the birds and bar-shaped F pieces become dominant (figure 4-49). The reader is encouraged to try different colors and depths of color on graph paper with colored markers until a pleasing balance is achieved.

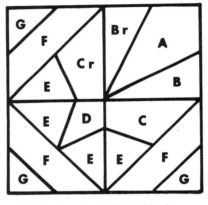

4-49. Twelve-inch Quilt Block.

MATERIALS AND CUTTING CHART

Fabrics	Yardage	Cutting Instructions*
1. blue	⅜ yard	4A, 4D, 4C, 4Cr
2. white	⅞ yard	4B, 4Br, 28H
		Borders: 4 strips 2½ by 24½ inches (seams included on borders)
3. dark green	⅞ yard	16E, 4F, 8G, 28H
4. yellow	⅜ yard	8F, 4G, 4I, 4J
5. Backing	1¼ yard	

"r" indicates reverse side of the pattern.
¼-inch seam allowances are not included unless indicated.

*Note: Cut strips for borders across the grain of fabric before cutting out pattern pieces.

FINISHED SIZE: 36 BY 36 INCHES

PIECING INSTRUCTIONS

1. Using the Pattern Pieces provided, trace and cut pieces according to the Cutting Instructions. Add ¼ inch seam allowances before cutting.

2. Sew B and Br to A (figure 4-50).

3. Sew G to F and C to E. Join units GF and CE (figure 4-51).

4. Repeat above directions for GF and CrE.

5. Sew G to F and both E pieces to D. Then join the GF unit to the EDE unit (figure 4-52).

6. Join four quarter-blocks to form the 12-inch block according to the diagram. Construct three more 12-inch blocks and sew together to form the design as illustrated in the Color Placement Guide.

7. For border 1: stitch white border strips to top and bottom of the design. Press. Attach I squares to each end of the two remaining white border strips. Sew to the sides of the design. Press.

8. For border 2: join white H to green H on diagonal sides. Repeat six more times (figure 4-53). Sew seven HH units together and attach to the top of the quilt. Repeat for the bottom. Press. Repeat for the sides, but sew J squares to each end of the HH borders before attaching to the quilt. Press.

4-47. **Birds of a Feather.** Designed by Sarah Doolan Gobes.

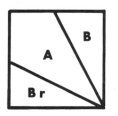

4-50. Piecing together B, Br, and A.

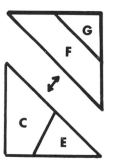

4-51. Piecing together G and F; piecing together C and E. Piece units together.

4-52. Piecing together two Es and D; piecing together EED and FG.

4-53. Piecing together Border 2.

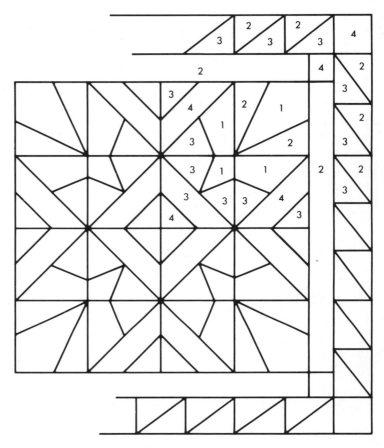

4-48. Color Placement Guide.

QUILTING

Layer and baste to prepare for quilting.

The quilting lines are indicated on the templates by broken lines. Where not indicated, the pieces are either outline quilted or quilted within the seam lines. Border 1 is quilted with zigzag lines. Use H template to mark this design for hand quilting. The hand quilting is, of course, optional and the reader is encouraged to incorporate original designs.

FINISHING

This quilt is finished with a 1¼-inch self-binding. The backing has been brought to the front, turned under, and blindstitched; and the corners have been mitered. See page 29 for complete instructions for this method of binding.

Birds of a Feather is a relatively simple design to machine or hand piece, containing only sixteen pieces per block. Its versatility and attractiveness will become evident when the reader experiments with different colorations and sets. Forty-eight blocks set together in rows of six by eight would make a single-bed quilt or a double-bed coverlet measuring 72 by 96 inches, not including the binding or optional borders.

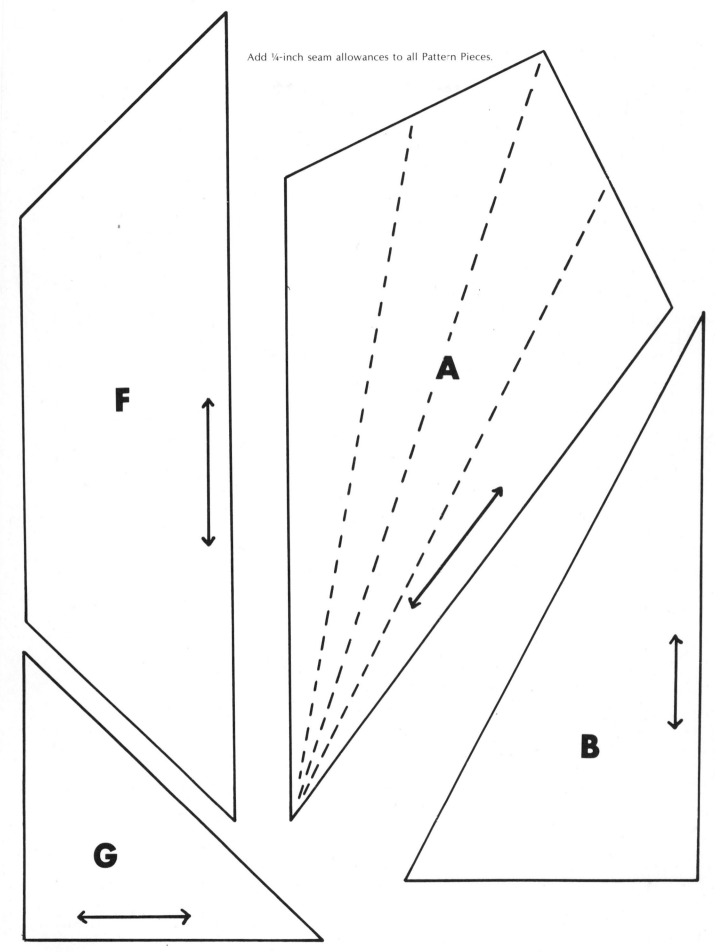

Add ¼-inch seam allowances to all Pattern Pieces.

F

A

B

G

4-54. Pattern Pieces.

Add ¼-inch seam allowances to all Pattern Pieces.

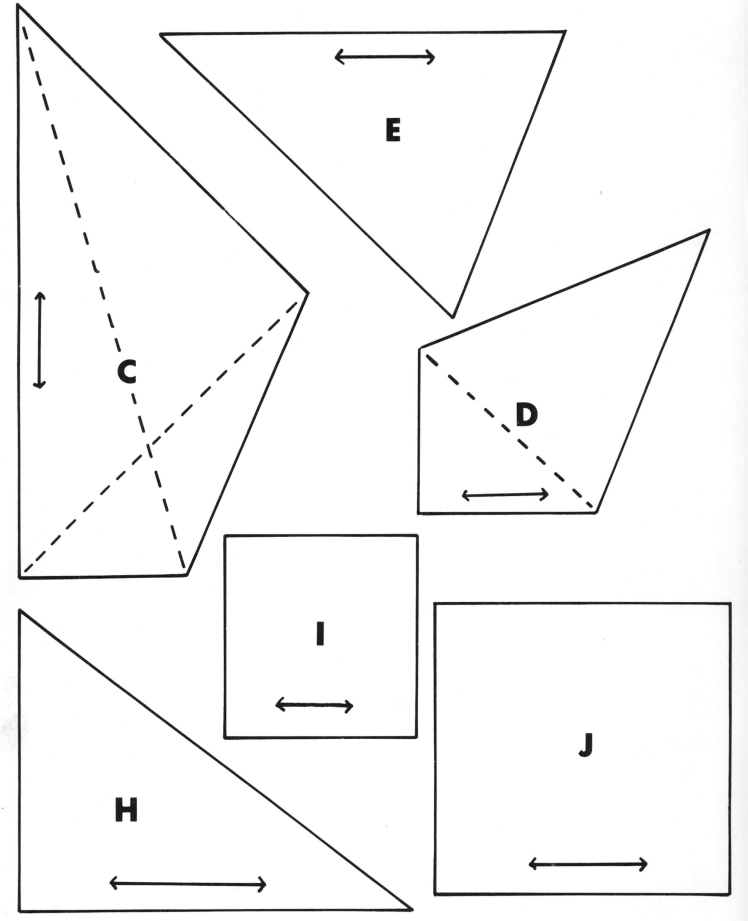

4-54. Pattern Pieces.

SKYSCRAPERS

Skyscrapers is a three-dimensional wall quilt which suggests an aerial view of a neatly planned city. The use of off-white, two shades of gray, and navy blue contributes to its citylike appearance. The checkerboard second border of Seminole patchwork is appropriate because it provides a bold frame for the quilt and also echoes, on a smaller scale, the navy and white squares in the design. This is an easy design to piece, even though the C squares must be carefully set in. Its contemporary look could be effectively achieved using other color combinations, but it is important to use light, medium, and dark tones on the B, Br, and C pieces for **Sky-scrapers** to have a three-dimensional quality.

MATERIALS AND CUTTING CHART

Fabric	Yardage	Cutting Instructions*
1. off-white	1 yard	16A, 16Ar, 8C
		5 strips 1⅝ by 45 inches cut across the grain for border 2 (seams included on borders)
2. medium gray	⅜ yard	16B
3. light gray	1¼ yard	16Br
		4 strips for border 1: 2 strips 2 by 28½ inches, 2 strips 2 by 31½ inches
		4 strips for border 3: 2 strips 4½ by 35 inches, 2 strips 4½ by 43½ inches (seams included on borders)
4. navy blue	⅜ yard	8C, five strips 1⅝ by 45 inches cut across the grain for border 2 (seams included on borders)
5. Backing	1¼ yard	

"r" indicates reverse side of the pattern.
¼-inch seam allowances are not included unless indicated.

*Note: Seam allowances are included on border strips. Cut these strips across the grain of the fabric before cutting out Pattern Pieces. This quilt has no binding because it is attached to stretcher frames.

FINISHED SIZE: 40 BY 40 INCHES

PIECING INSTRUCTIONS

1. Using the Pattern Pieces provided, trace and cut pieces according to the Cutting Instructions. Add ¼-inch seam allowances before cutting.
2. Sew A to B, and Ar to Br (figure 4-57). Join the AB section to the ArBr section. Set in the C square to complete the block (figure 4-58).
3. Construct each of the sixteen blocks in the same manner, piecing eight blocks with navy C pieces, and eight with white C pieces (figure 4-59).
4. Consulting the Color Placement Guide, sew the blocks together in rows of four, and then sew the four rows together to complete the design.
5. Attach border 1 to the top and bottom of the design. Press. Attach side border strips. Press. Repeat for borders 2 and 3.

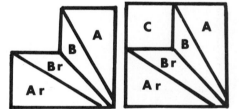

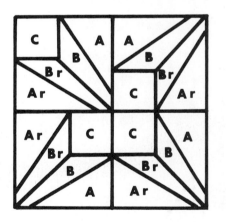

4-57. Piecing together A, B, Br, and Ar.
4-58. Adding C.
4-59. Piecing the block together.

4-55. **Skyscrapers.** Designed by Sarah Doolan Gobes.

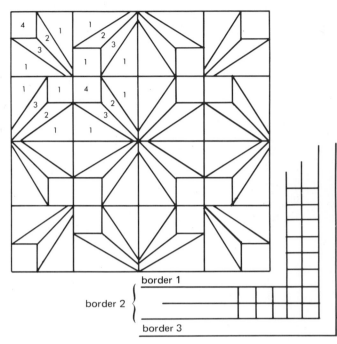

4-56. Color Placement Guide.

Seminole Border 2 Instructions

Cut strips 1⅝ inches wide across the grain of the white and navy fabrics. Sew together one navy and one white strip (figure 4-60). Press seam to one side. Repeat for other four pairs of strips. Cut band into 1⅝-inch segments (figure 4-61) and stitch so that colors alternate in checkerboard fashion (figure 4-62). Top and bottom Seminole bands will be 29 squares wide, side bands will be 33 squares wide. Since some fabrics stretch and seam allowances may vary slightly, ease the band to fit border 1.

QUILTING

The hand quilting on **Skyscrapers** consists of straight lines which echo the sides of the B and Br pieces and extend through the borders. Use a compass to form a circular quilting line on the C squares.

FINISHING

This wall quilt is mounted on 40-inch stretcher frames. See page 37 for instructions on mounting and finishing.

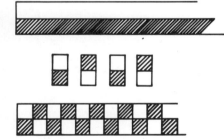

4-60. Sewing strips together.
4-61. Cutting band into segments.
4-62. Piecing segments together.

Add ¼-inch seam allowances to all Pattern Pieces.

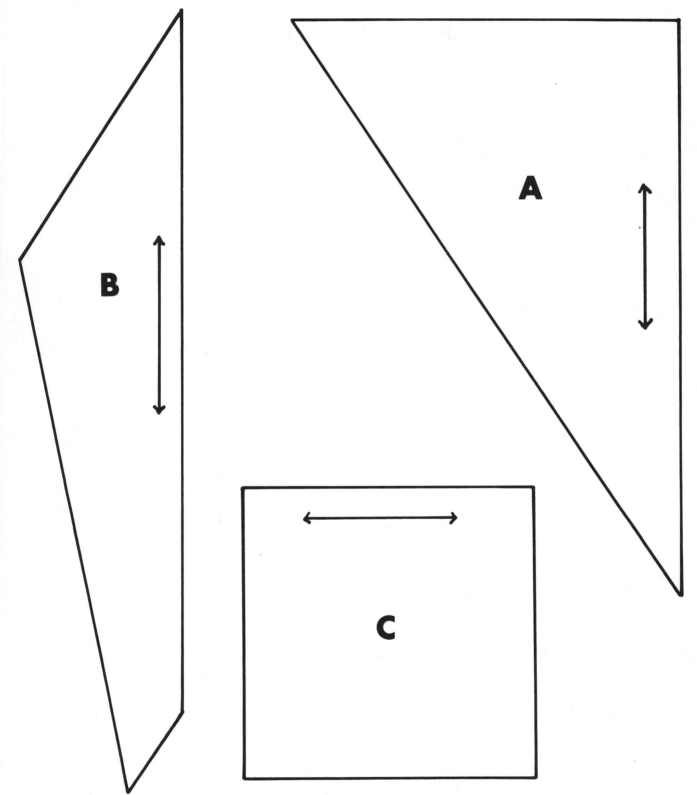

4-63 Pattern Pieces.

INTERSTICES

Interstices is a bold graphic design consisting of overlapping squares in vibrant colors. The squares appear to be superimposed on a background of off-white with certain areas shaded in light gray and black. A contemporary design, **Interstices** is intended to be framed with a purchased metal frame. It has been layered with batting, but there is no quilting.

The sewing is simple and the project may be machine pieced, but because the colors change from block to block, the Color Placement Guide must be consulted to facilitate piecing. You might find it helpful to trace the Guide and fill in the colors with felt-tip pens.

MATERIALS AND CUTTING CHART

Fabrics	Yardage	Cutting Instructions*
1. white	½ yard	8A, 6C, 12D, 6F, 6G
2. black	¼ yard	2C, 4D
3. light gray	¼ yard	3A, 2D, 2G
4. medium gray	⅜ yard	2 strips 2½ by 24½ inches, 2 strips 2½ by 28½ inches (seams included on borders)
5. pink	¼ yard	4B, 2E, 2Er, 2H, 2Hr
6. purple	¼ yard	6B, 1E, 1H, 1Hr
7. dark red	⅝ yard	6B, 1E, 1H, 1Hr
		2 strips 4¼ by 28½ inches, 2 strips 4¼ by 36 inches (seams included on borders)

"r" indicates reverse side of the pattern.
¼-inch seam allowances are not included unless indicated.

*Note: Cut strips for borders across the grain of fabric before cutting pattern pieces. The first border is medium gray, the second one is dark red. Two inches of extra fabric has been allowed on the red border to be wrapped to the back of piece for mounting.

FINISHED SIZE: 32 BY 32 INCHES

PIECING INSTRUCTIONS

1. Using the Pattern Pieces provided, trace and cut pieces according to the Cutting Instructions. Add ¼ inch for seam allowances before cutting.

2. Join A to B to C. Piece eight blocks in this manner, consulting Color Placement Guide and photo for correct color combinations (figure 4-67).

3. Join D, E, and F. Join G, H, and D. Sew the DEF and GHD units to the B piece, consulting Color Placement Guide and Piecing Together Diagrams. Construct four blocks in this manner (figure 4-68).

4. Construct two blocks as shown, but join F, Er, and D, and D, Hr, and G to the B piece.

5. Join two D pieces. Join D to Hr to G. Sew the DD unit and the DHrG unit to the B piece. Construct two blocks in this manner (figure 4-69).

4-64. Interstices. Designed by Sarah Doolan Gobes.

6. Attach blocks together in rows of four horizontally. Sew the four rows together according to the Piecing Diagram.

7. Attach border 1 to the top and bottom, and then to the sides. Repeat for border 2.

FINISHING

See page 37 for instructions on how to prepare the piece for a purchased frame.

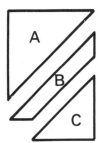

4-67

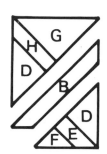

4-68

4-67. Piecing together A, B, and C.
4-68. Piecing together G, H, and D; piecing together E, F, and D. Join both units to B.
4-69. Piecing together two Ds; piecing together G, Hr, and D. Join both units to B.

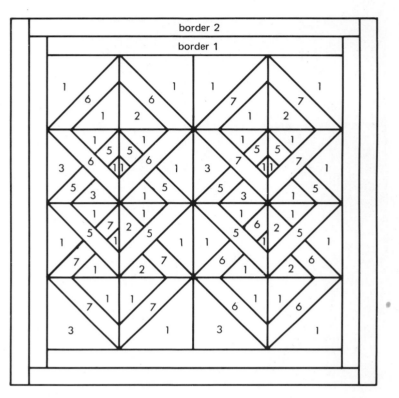

4-65. Color Placement Guide.

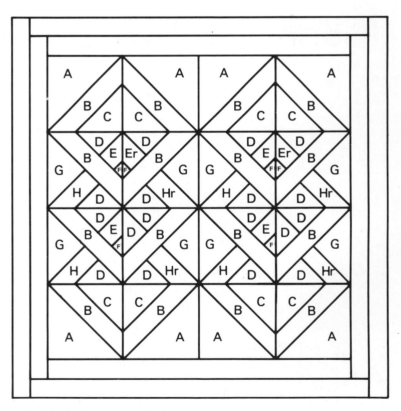

4-66. Block Placement Guide.

Add ¼-inch seam allowances to all Pattern Pieces.

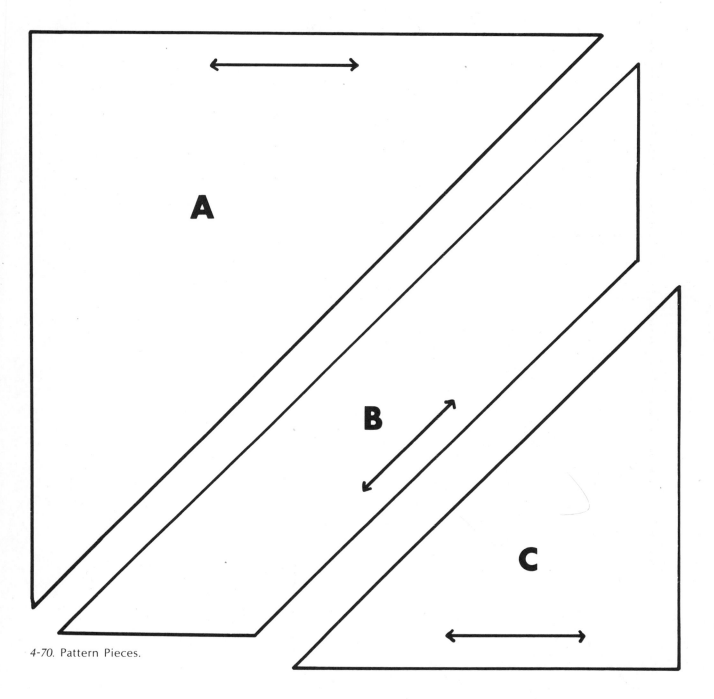

4-70. Pattern Pieces.

Add ¼-inch seam allowances to all Pattern Pieces.

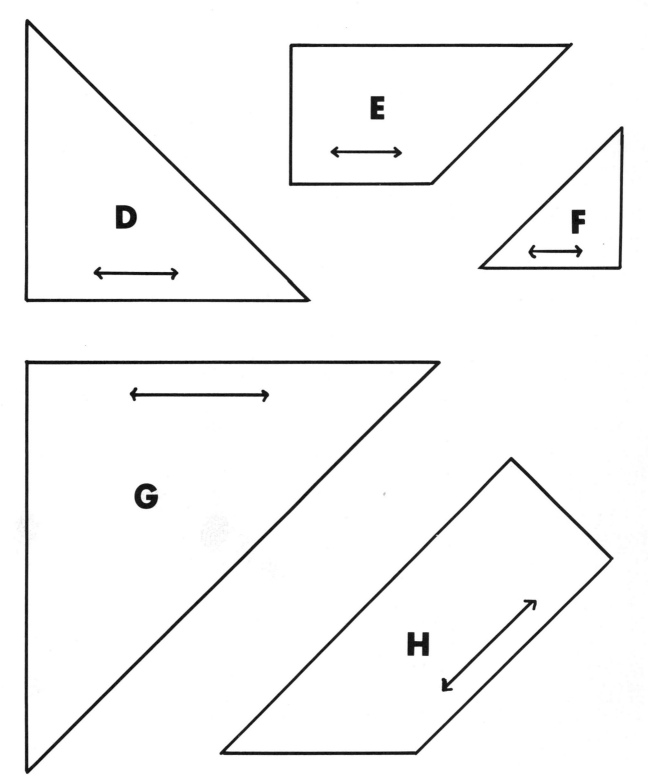

4-70. Pattern Pieces.

SEMINOLE STAR

Sometimes the design for a wall quilt is the result of experimentation with a particular technique. Books on Seminole patchwork suggest ways to use these decorative bands on linens and garments, but few, if any, use them in wall hangings. **Seminole Star** evolved from a desire to combine a sampling of these colorful bands with pieced sections and hand quilting. The Seminole panels radiate from the points of an off-center gold star, and they alternate with geometric shapes of dark solid colors.

Seminole Star will appeal to the person who loves this type of patchwork and is looking for new ways to use the technique. These instructions may be followed explicitly, or they may be used as a general guide, substituting other types of Seminole bands, or plain strips of fabric. The result will be an example of personal expression using a technique that has unlimited possibilities.

The novice should experiment and practice with Seminole bands to master the technique before attempting this particular design. It might also be helpful to trace and color the graph of the design to facilitate piecing and color placement.

4-71. **Seminole Star.** Designed by Sarah Doolan Gobes.

95

MATERIALS AND CUTTING CHART

Fabrics	Yardage	Cutting Instructions*
1. gold	¼ yard	1A, 4B
2. navy blue	⅜ yard	2 triangles from Color Placement Guide
3. purple	¼ yard	4 shapes from Guide
4. black	⅞ yard	2 triangles from Guide
		Borders: 2 strips 1½ by
		28½ inches, 2 strips 1½ by 24½ inches
		Binding: 2 strips 1½ by 37½ inches,
		2 strips 1½ by 31½ inches
5. royal blue	¼ yard	Borders: 2 strips 1½ by 28½ inches, 2 strips 1½ by 24½ inches (seams included on borders and bindings)
6. Seminole	1 to 1½ yards	assorted colors of new or scrap fabric for the four Seminole panels in Color Placement Guide.
7. Backing	1 yard	

"r" indicates reverse side of the pattern
¼-inch seam allowances are not included unless indicated.

*Note: Cut strips for borders and bindings across the grain of the fabric before cutting out pattern pieces.

FINISHED SIZE: 31 BY 37 INCHES

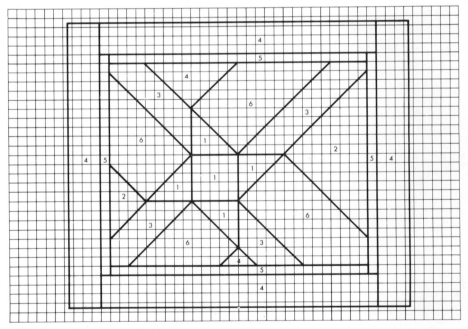

4-72. Color Placement Guide.

PIECING INSTRUCTIONS

1. On a piece of posterboard that measures 22 by 28 inches, draw lines horizontally and vertically in a 1-inch grid. Each square of the grid on the Color Placement Guide represents 1 square inch on the posterboard.

2. Draw lines on posterboard to correspond to design lines on the Guide.

Label all Pattern Pieces and cut apart to use as templates. (Borders will be added when design is complete and are not drawn on posterboard.)

3. Trace and cut fabric pieces for solid-colored shapes, adding ¼-inch seam allowances. Set aside and prepare Seminole bands.

4. Seminole band instructions:

Pattern A: checkerboard design. Cut 1¼-inch-wide strips of each of two colors. Follow sewing instructions in **Skyscrapers** project for Seminole checkerboard design, but cut segments 1¼-inches wide. Press seams to one side.

Pattern B: zigzag band in three colors. Cut strips 1½, ¾, and 1½ inches wide across the grain. Stitch together with the narrowest band in the middle. Mark with pencil and ruler, then cut 1½-inch segments on the diagonal, indenting 2½ inches on the top to achieve the appropriate diagonal slant (figure 4-73). Repeat these directions for a second band, but reverse the diagonal slant. Cut segments apart and resew, alternating one segment from the first band and one from the second so that the middle strip forms the zigzag (figure 4-74). Press seams to one side.

Pattern C: triangles in two colors. Cut 1¾-inch strips of each of two colors. Sew and press. Cut into 1½-inch segments. Resew, off-setting each segment by 1 inch (figure 4-75). Press seams to one side and trim band on broken lines as indicated.

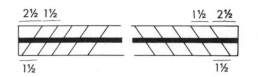
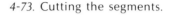

4-73. Cutting the segments.

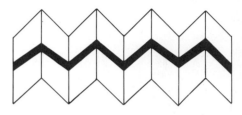

4-74. Piecing the segments together.

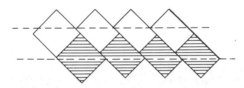

4-75. Off-setting each segment by 1 inch.

Pattern D: diagonal checkerboard. Cut 2-inch strips of each of two colors. Sew and cut into 2-inch segments on the diagonal, indenting 2½ inches on the top to achieve the appropriate diagonal slant (figure 4-76). Turn every other segment upside down and sew so that the center seam lines match. Press seams to one side.

Prepare a variety of Seminole bands using these or other patterns. Piece them as necessary to make them desired length.

5. Cut narrow strips of plain or printed fabric ¾ inch wide, and also cut some that are 1 inch wide. Sew one or more plain strips to each Seminole band, alternating bands and colors for variety. Sew together as many Seminole bands and plain strips of fabric as necessary to make a panel wide enough to cut out templates for each of the four Seminole sections in Color Placement Guide. Add seam allowances to the Seminole sections. Note: It is difficult to estimate yardage for Seminole patchwork because widths of bands and segments vary, and therefore the lengths of the bands are not equal. It may be necessary to piece together some bands to achieve the desired length. Since this design consists of a variety of colors and patterns, you can easily use scraps and leftover fabric. It is also possible to use plain or printed strips of fabric in various widths instead of the Seminole bands.

6. Stitch gold B pieces to ends of each purple shape.

4-76. Cutting the segments.

4-77. Piecing the segments together.

7. Seam large solid shapes and gold/purple units to the sides of each Seminole panel.

8. Join the Seminole/plain sections, and carefully set in the center gold square. Press carefully to avoid stretching the bias.

9. Attach narrow royal blue borders to top and bottom. Press. Repeat for the sides.

10. Attach the wide black borders to the top and bottom. Press. Repeat for the sides. Layer and baste.

QUILTING

Hand quilting lines for the gold star are indicated by broken lines on the templates. The large zigzag quilting design is also provided and may be used within the large plain shapes, or an original design may be substituted. The borders have been left unquilted.

FINISHING

Attach the narrow black binding to the top and bottom, press, then repeat for the sides. See page 27 for instructions on binding. The finished binding is ½ inch wide. **Seminole Star** has sleeves sewn to the top and bottom (see page 35 for instructions). Firring strips have been inserted to facilitate hanging.

Add ¼-inch seam allowances to all Pattern Pieces.

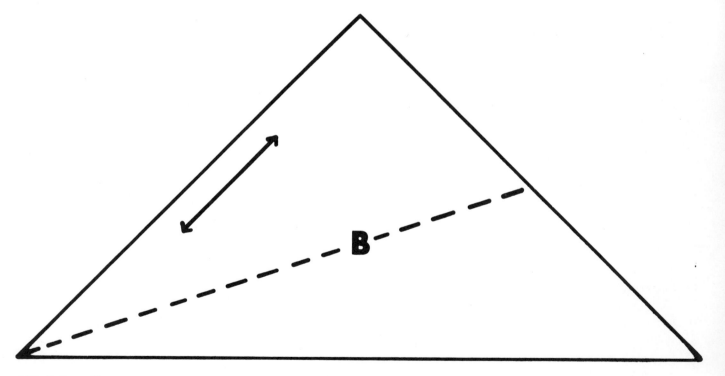

4-78. Pattern Pieces.

Add ¼-inch seam allowances to all Pattern Pieces.

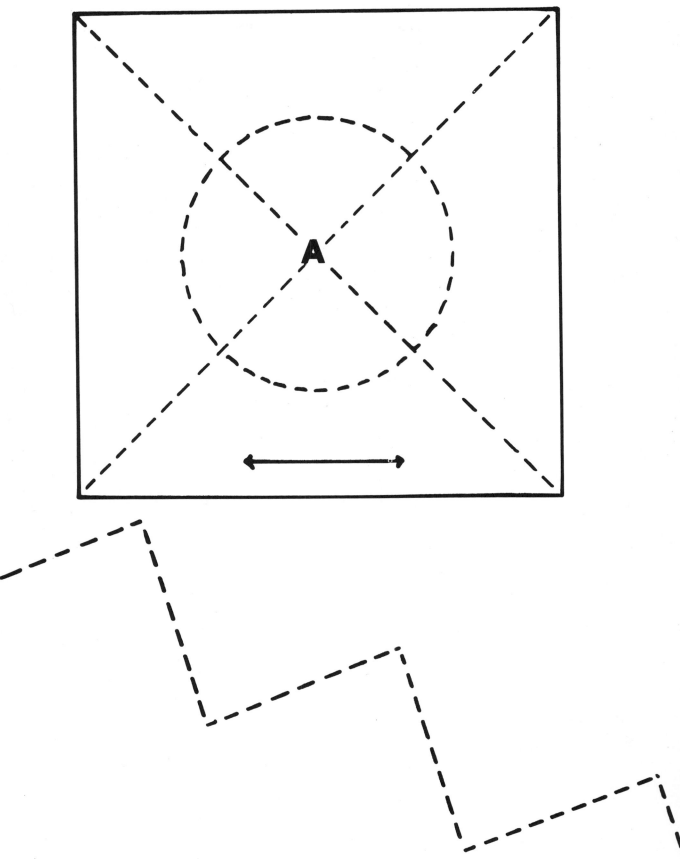

PERPETUAL MOTION

Both the primary and secondary designs in this quilt are spinning, slowing down only when some of the colored pieces are deleted at the outer edges of the quilt. The name comes from a piece by the same name in the Suzuki violin repertoire in which the melody builds and repeats and seems to be in constant rotation.

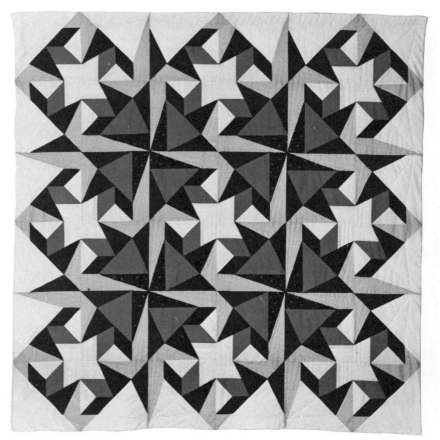

4-79. **Perpetual Motion.** Designed by Sheila Meyer.

MATERIALS AND CUTTING CHART

Fabrics	Yardage	Cutting Instructions
1. dark print	⅓ yard	16F
2. dark print coordinated	1½ yards	36A, 36C
3. pumpkin	1½ yards	36B, 16E
4. champagne	2¼ yards	36D, 24G, 12J
5. rust	⅔ yard	24Dr
6. off-white	2¾ yards	36H, 36I, 8K, 8L, 4M
7. Backing + binding	4¼ yards	

"r" indicates the reverse side of the pattern.
¼-inch seam allowances are not included.

FINISHED SIZE: 72 BY 72 INCHES

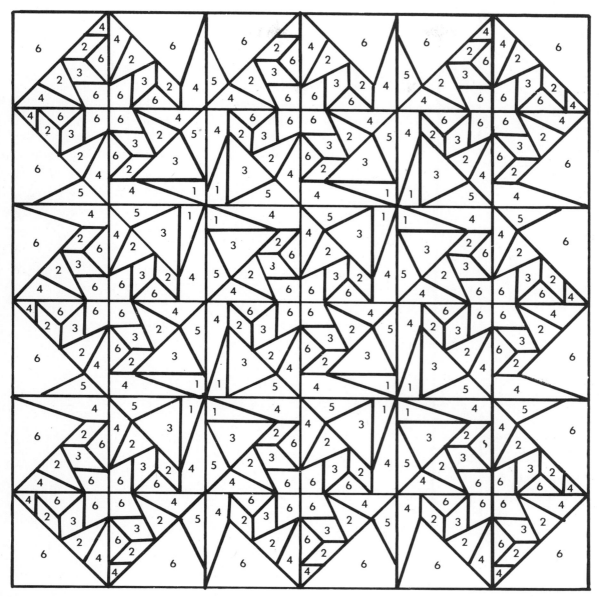

4-80. Color Placement Guide.

PIECING INSTRUCTIONS

1. Using the Pattern Pieces provided, trace and cut pieces according to the Cutting Instructions. Add ¼-inch seam allowances before cutting.

2. Sew an A to a B (figure 4-86).

3. Set in an I (figure 4-87).

4. Add an H along the free side of the B (figure 4-88).

5. Join a C to a D (figure 4-89).

6. Bring these two units together and sew (figure 4-90).

7. Now sew an E to a Dr (figure 4-91).

8. Sew this unit to the one completed in step 6 (figure 4-92).

9. Now sew a G to an F (figure 4-93).

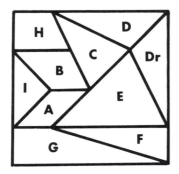

4-81. **W** block.

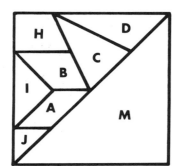

4-82. **X** block.

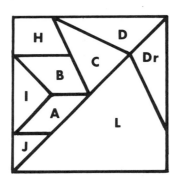

4-83. **Y** block.

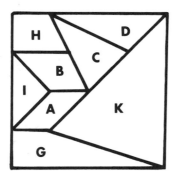

4-84. **Z** block.

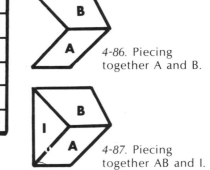

4-85. Block Placement Guide.

4-86. Piecing together A and B.

4-87. Piecing together AB and I.

10. Sew this to the unit completed in Step 8 (figure 4-94).

11. Repeat Steps 2 through 10 fifteen times, thereby completing the 16**W** blocks that form the core of the design.

12. To make the four **X** corner blocks, follow Steps 2 through 6.

13. Then sew a J to this unit along the free side of the A (figure 4-95).

14. Now sew an M (one half of a 12-inch square) to the unit completed in Step 13 (figure 4-96).

15. Repeat Steps 12 through 14 three times, completing the four **X** blocks.

16. To make the **Y** blocks, follow Steps 2 through 6. Then add a J as in step 13 (figure 4-97).

17. Sew a Dr to an L (figure 4-97).

18. Join this unit to the one completed in Step 16 (figure 4-98).

19. Repeat Steps 16 through 18 seven times.

20. To make the **Z** blocks follow Steps 2 through 6.

21. Attach this to a K (figure 4-99).

22. Set in a G to complete this block (figure 4-100).

23. Repeat steps 20 through 22 seven times. Now you should have 16**W**, 4**X**, 8**Y**, and 8**Z** blocks.

24. Lay out these blocks and sew together according to the Color Placement Guide.

QUILTING

Mark for quilting using the dotted lines on the Pattern Pieces. Add more lines if you prefer denser quilting.

Layer the quilt, using directions given (see page 23). Quilt as marked.

FINISHING

Bind the edges, following the method described on page 29 as *invisible binding* using separate binding strips.

VARIATIONS

This quilt can easily be made larger to accommodate to bed sizes. Add enough of the center **X** blocks for the required measurements. Then add the necessary number of **Y** and **Z** blocks to the sides to adjust for the new dimensions.

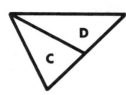

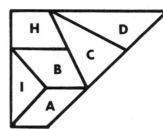

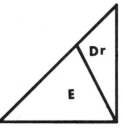

4-88. Piecing together ABI and H.

4-89. Piecing together C and D.

4-90. Piecing together the two units.

4-91. Piecing together E and Dr.

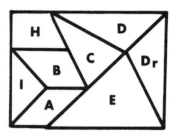

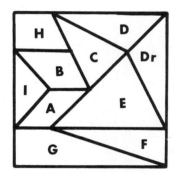

4-92. Piecing together Edr and the larger unit.

4-93. Piecing together G and F.

4-94. Completed **W** block.

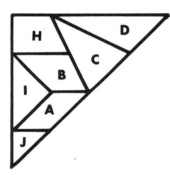

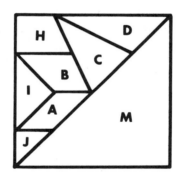

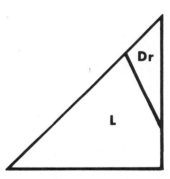

4-95. Piecing together J and larger unit.

4-96. Completed **X** block.

4-97. Piecing together Dr and L.

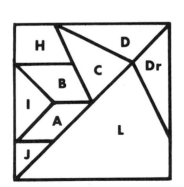

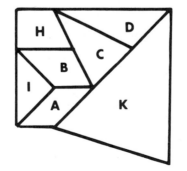

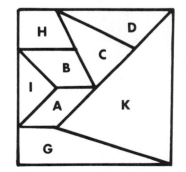

4-98. Completed **Y** block.

4-99. Piecing together K and larger unit.

4-100. Completed **Z** block.

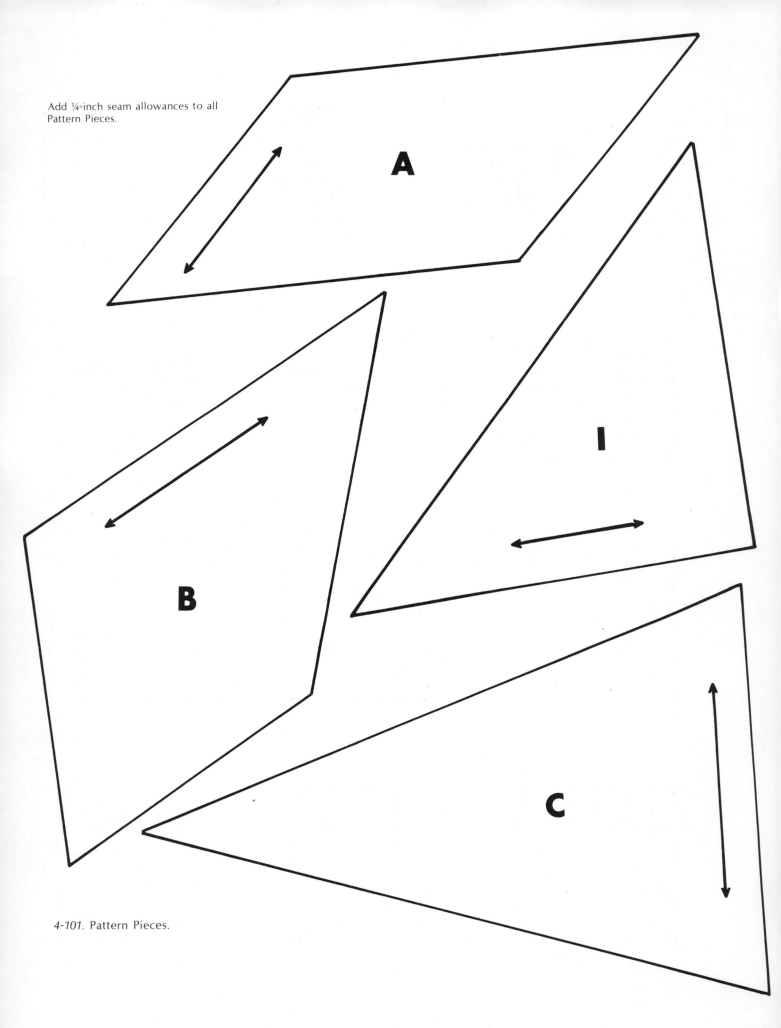

Add ¼-inch seam allowances to all Pattern Pieces.

A

B

I

C

4-101. Pattern Pieces.

Dotted lines inside Pattern Piece indicate quilting lines.
Add ¼-inch seam allowances to all Pattern Pieces.
"r" indicates the reverse side of the pattern.

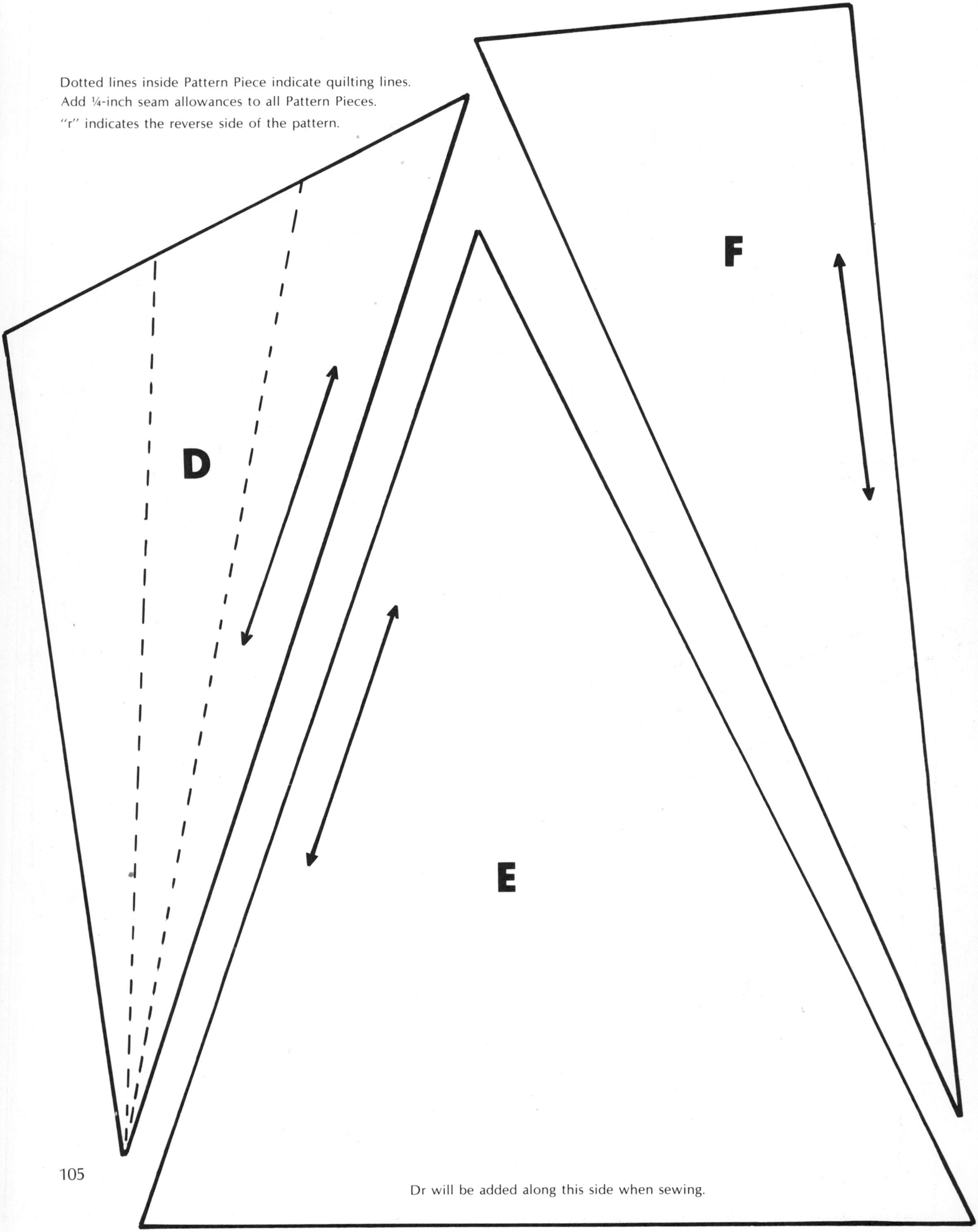

D

F

E

Dr will be added along this side when sewing.

Tape pieces together at dotted line xy to form Pattern Piece G.

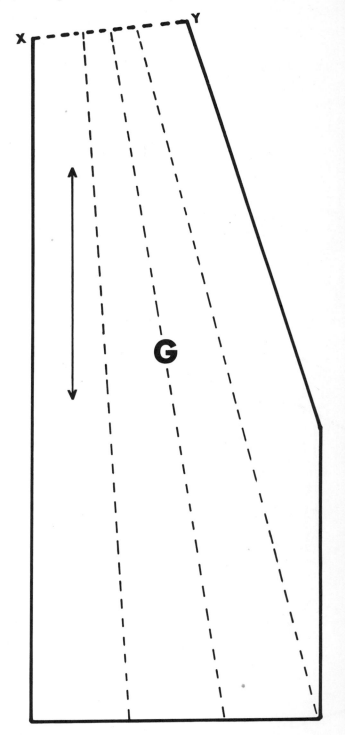

Add ¼-inch seam allowances to all Pattern Pieces.

Dotted lines inside indicate quilting lines.

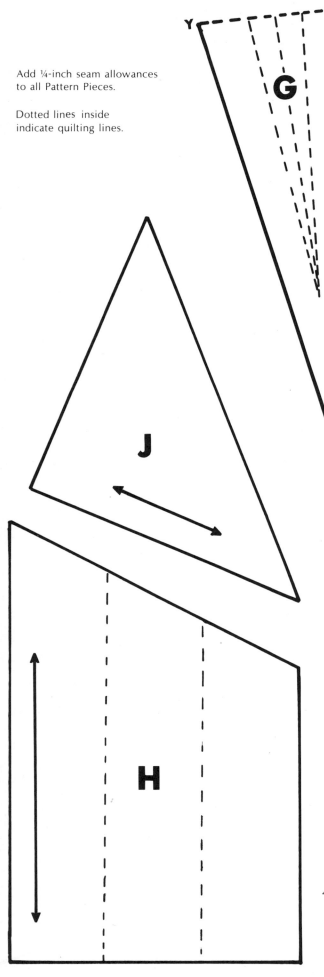

G

J

H

M To make Pattern Piece M, draw a 12-inch square and cut it in half diagonally.

4-101. Pattern Pieces.

Tape pieces together at dotted lines to form Pattern Piece K.
Add ¼-inch seam allowance at solid lines.

K

4-101. Pattern Pieces.

Add ¼-inch seam allowance at solid lines.

Tape pieces together at dotted lines
to form Pattern Piece L.
When complete, Pattern Piece L
should look like this.

L

L

4-101. Pattern Pieces.

ECHO

In this quilt stark contrasting fabrics are used to convey the feeling of vibrations. The use of opposing colors on the color wheel will also create intense vibrations, whereas the use of complementary or muted colors will alter this effect.

4-102. **Echo.** Designed by Sheila Meyer.

MATERIALS AND CUTTING CHART

Fabrics	Yardage	Cutting Instructions
1. black	1¾ yards	4A, 8Ar, 8B, 8Br, 4C, 4E 2 strips 35½ by 3 inches, 2 strips 40½ by 3 inches (seams included) 4 strips 2½ by 15 inches, 4 strips 2½ by 12½ inches Binding strips: leave piece 6 inches by 45 inches uncut
2. ivory	1 yard	20B, 20Br, 4D 4 strips 2½ by 10 inches, 4 strips 2½ by 5 inches, 8 strips 2½ by 7½ inches
3. Backing	1¼ yards	

"r" indicates the reverse side of the pattern.
¼-inch seam allowances are not included unless indicated.

FINISHED SIZE: 40 BY 40 INCHES

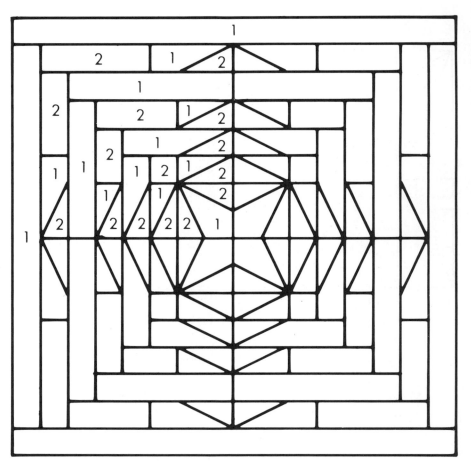

4-103. Color Placement Guide.

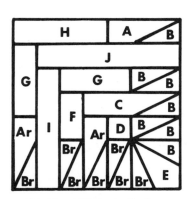

4-104. The 17½-inch Quilt
Block.

PIECING INSTRUCTIONS

1. Trace Pattern Pieces and cut according to the Cutting Instructions. Use the Quilt Block (figure 4-104) as a guide to the placement of Pattern Pieces and match colors according to the Color Placement Guide. Add ¼-inch seam allowances before cutting.

2. Sew an ivory B and Br onto an E as shown in figure 4-105.

3. Sew an ivory Br to a black Br and sew onto the side of the block (figure 4-106). Now sew an ivory B to a black B and join to an ivory D. Attach as shown in figure 4-106, across the top of the block.

4. Sew a black Ar to an ivory Br and attach to the side of the block (figure 4-107). Sew a black C to an ivory B and attach across the top.

5. Sew a black Br to an ivory Br. Add this to a 2½- by 5-inch ivory strip and sew down the side of the block (figure 4-108). Sew a black B to an ivory B and attach this to a 2½- by 7½-inch ivory strip. Sew this across the top of the block (figure 4-108).

6. Attach a black 2½- by 12½-inch strip to the side of the block and a 2½ by 15-inch strip across the top (figure 4-109).

7. Sew a black Ar to an ivory Br and attach to an ivory 2½- by 7½-inch strip. Sew this down the side as shown in figure 4-110. Then join a black A

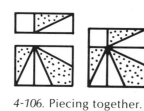
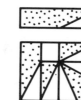
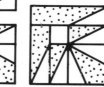

4-105. Piecing together.

4-106. Piecing together.

4-107. Piecing together.

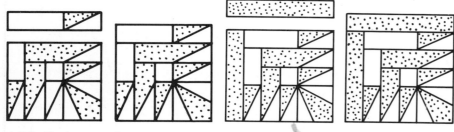

4-108. Piecing together.

4-109. Piecing together.

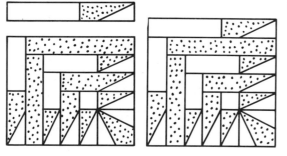

4-110. Piecing together.

to an ivory B and sew onto an ivory 2½- by 10-inch strip. Sew this across the top of the block (figure 4-110).

8. Make three more squares following Steps 2 through 7.

9. Join these four squares together using the Color Placement Guide.

10. Sew the two black 3- by 35½-inch strips (seams included) down the sides of the quilt. Then add the two black 3- by 40½-inch strips (seams included) across the top and bottom.

QUILTING

Any visible quilting will soften the sharpness of the contrast in this piece. By *quilting in the ditch* you can preserve the hard lines. If you would prefer softer lines, try a quilting design or quilt ¼ inch in from the seam lines. Mark the quilting lines with a hard lead pencil.

Layer and baste the quilt (see page 23). Quilt as marked.

FINISHING

Bind in black, using the separate binding method (see page 27).

111

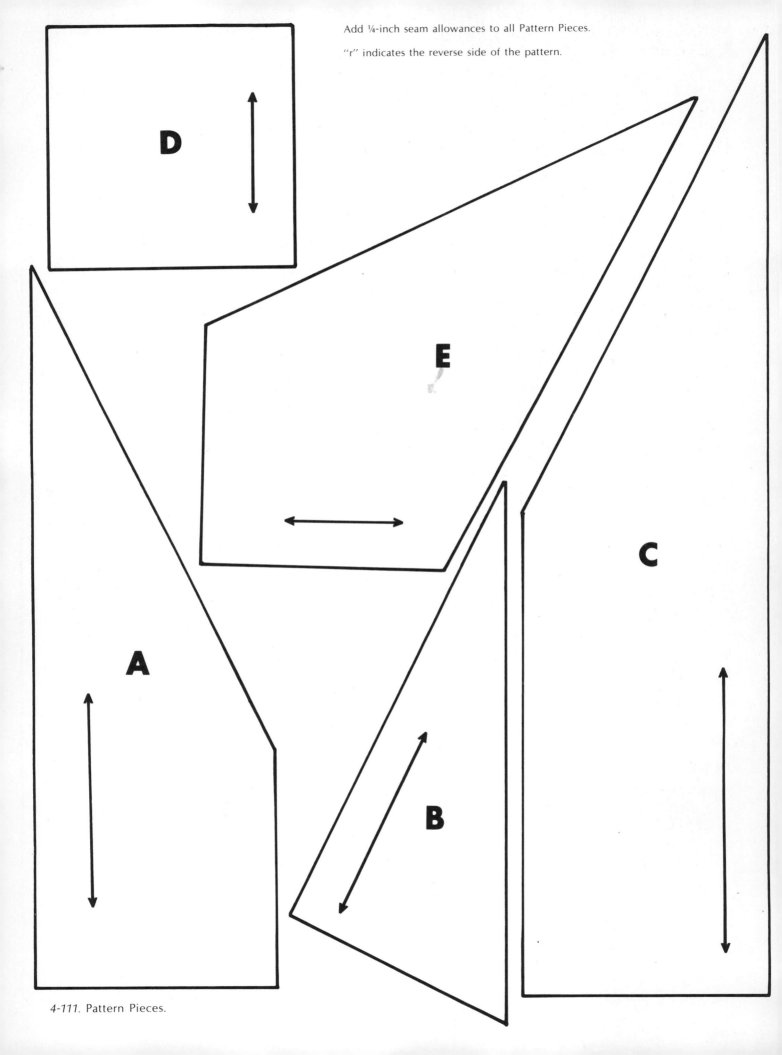

Add ¼-inch seam allowances to all Pattern Pieces.

"r" indicates the reverse side of the pattern.

D

E

A

B

C

4-111. Pattern Pieces.

Add ¼-inch seam allowances (at solid lines) to all Pattern Pieces.

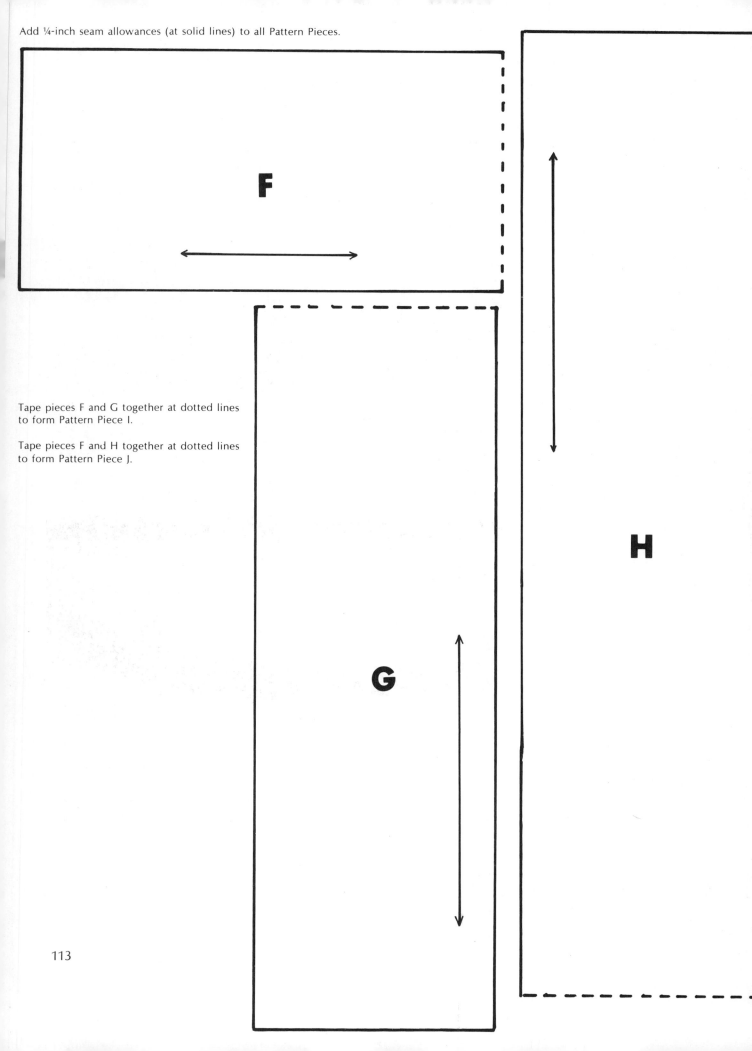

F

Tape pieces F and G together at dotted lines to form Pattern Piece I.

Tape pieces F and H together at dotted lines to form Pattern Piece J.

H

G

SPRING FLOWER

This design was inspired by the stylized flowers in many of the traditional quilts. The vivid colors of the flowers and leaves give a crisp look when contrasted against a white background. As a wall hanging or a bed quilt it can be the focal point in a room with contemporary decor. Muted or pastel colors change the effect completely, giving a soft, wistful impression.

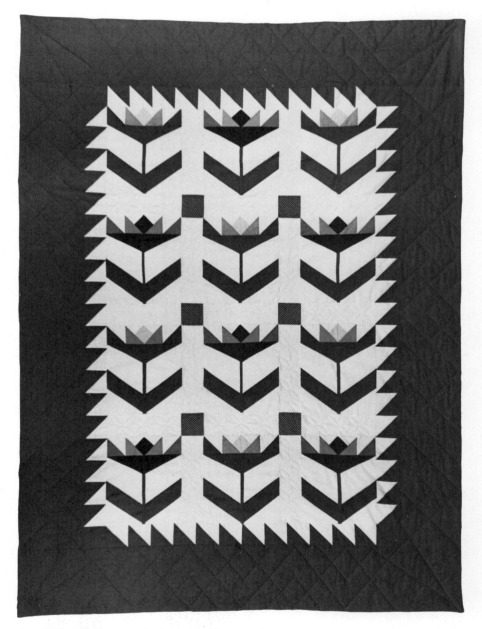

4-112. **Spring Flower.** Designed by Sheila Meyer.

4-113. Color Placement Guide.

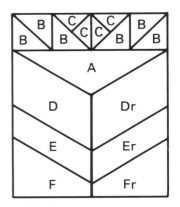

4-114. Ten-by-twelve-inch Quilt Block.

4-115. Piecing together two Bs.

4-116. Piecing together two Cs and B.

4-117. Piecing together the four squares.

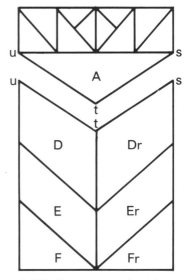

4-118. Piecing together the whole flowerhead.

MATERIALS AND CUTTING CHART

Fabrics	Yardage	Cutting Instructions
1. red	3 yards	6A, 12B, 62G, 4H
		2 strips 9½ by 60½ inches, 2 strips 9½ by 62½ inches (seams included)
2. white	3 yards	24B, 24C, 12D, 12Dr, 12F, 12Fr, 62G
		8 strips 3½ by 12½ inches, 9 strips 3½ by 10½ inches (seams included)
3. green	¾ yard	12E, 12Er
		12 strips 1 by 7½ inch (seams included)
4. green dot	¼ yard	6H
5. purple	¼ yard	6A, 12C
6. lavender	¼ yard	12B
7. orange	¼ yard	12B
8. yellow	¼ yard	12C
9. salmon	¼ yard	12B
10. Backing + binding	5 yards	

"r" indicates the reverse side of the pattern.
¼-inch seam allowances are not included unless indicated.

FINISHED SIZE: 60 BY 80 INCHES

PIECING INSTRUCTIONS

1. Using the Pattern Pieces provided, trace and cut pieces according to the Cutting Instructions Add ¼-inch seam allowances before cutting.

2. Except for the color of the flower base (A) and petals (B and C) all twelve design blocks are identical (figure 4-114). To begin, sew a white B to a red B to form a square (figure 4-115).

3. Sew a white C to a yellow C to form a triangle. Sew this to an orange B (figure 4-116) to form a square.

4. Repeat Steps 2 and 3, reversing the position of the two C triangles (figure 4-117).

5. Join these four squares to form the petals (figure 4-117).

6. Attach this row to the red A flower base, forming the whole flower head (figure 4-118).

7. Join D, E, and F. Repeat for the three reversed pieces Dr, Er, and Fr.

8. Sew these two units together down the center.

9. Make a stem by folding a 1- by 7½-inch strip of the leaf fabric (color 3). Fold under ¼ inch on each long side. Blindstitch this folded strip over the center seam of the DEF unit. Cut off excess.

10. Bring the flower head to the base unit. Pin along lines **s-t** and sew. Then pin from **t** to **u**, pivoting at the center point, and sew. This step is easier to do by hand.

11. Repeat the above Steps 2 through 10 for each of the remaining eleven flower blocks, substituting the purple block colors or your own color combinations.

12. Join the flower blocks and sashing strips according to the Color Placement Guide.

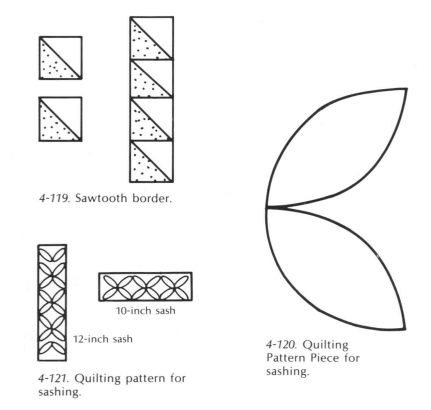

4-119. Sawtooth border.

10-inch sash

12-inch sash

4-121. Quilting pattern for sashing.

4-120. Quilting Pattern Piece for sashing.

13. To make sawtooth border, join a red G to a white G along the long sides to form a square (figure 4-119). Do this sixty-two times. Sew together two strips of twelve of these squares and add them to the top and bottom of the quilt. Sew together two strips of nineteen of these squares, adding a red H square at each end and sewing them down the sides of the quilt.

14. To make outer border, sew a 9½- by 62½-inch red strip onto each side of the quilt. Then sew a 9½- by 60½-inch red strip to the top and bottom. These strips have the seam allowances included in their measurements.

QUILTING

Use the petal pattern (figure 4-120) in the sashing on this quilt (figure 4-121), or you might prefer a precut stencil. A commercial stencil can also be used in the red border or you can create your own linear design. If you want more quilting, mark ¼ inch in from the seams in all of the white areas except the sashing.

Now you are ready to layer the quilt. See page 23 on layering. Quilt as marked.

FINISHING

Bind the edges using the method described in Chapter 1 as *invisible binding* using separate binding strips.

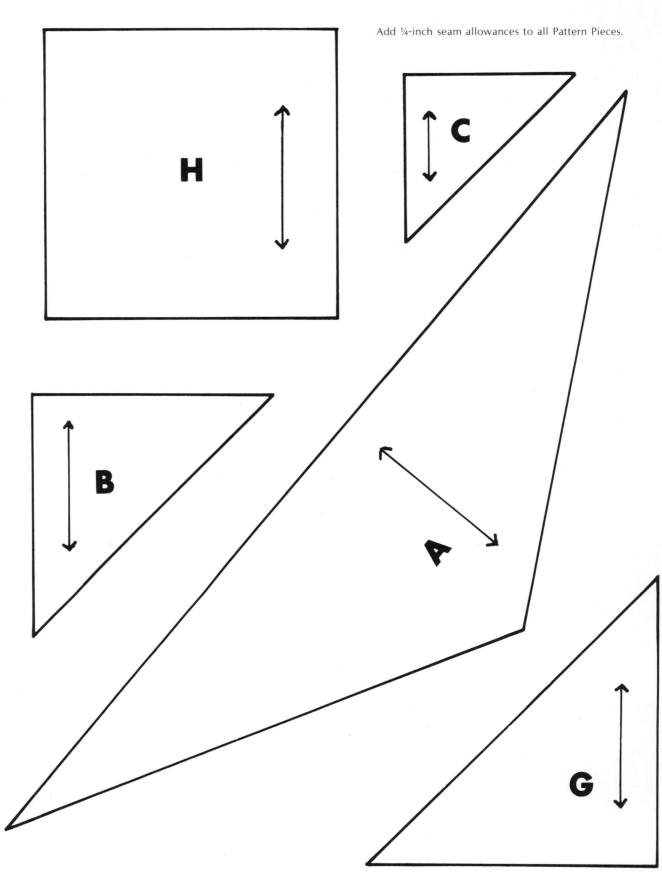

Add ¼-inch seam allowances to all Pattern Pieces.

4-122. Pattern Pieces.

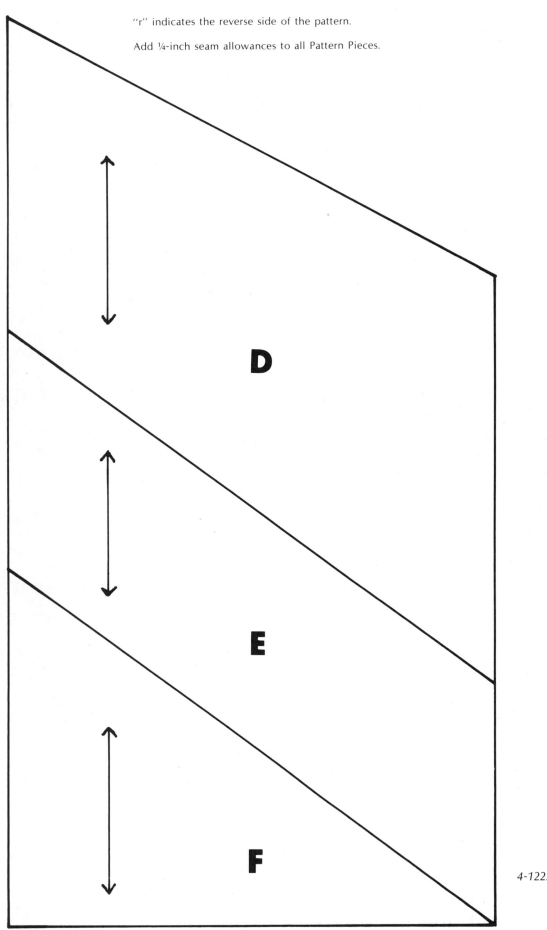

"r" indicates the reverse side of the pattern.

Add ¼-inch seam allowances to all Pattern Pieces.

D

E

F

4-122. Pattern Pieces.

INTERLOCKING STARS

There are several layers of stars in this design, seemingly superimposed upon each other. At times the stars appear independently and at others they seem to join together to form larger stars. There is a *Rob-Peter-to-Pay-Paul* effect where you borrow from one design to complete another. When set on the diagonal, the quilt is dynamic and has a great deal of movement. It is more controlled and the movement seems to slow down when it is placed straight up and down.

4-123. **Interlocking Stars.** Designed by Sheila Meyer.

MATERIALS AND CUTTING CHART

Fabrics	Yardage	Cutting Instructions
1. dark print	¾ yard	20A
2. dark print coordinated with color 1	1½ yards	16F, 64H, 4M 2 strips 1 by 45½ inches, 2 strips 1 by 46½ inches (seams included)
3. rust	½ yard	16A
4. medium brown print	1⅓ yards	36B
5. peach (terra cotta)	1½ yards	72C, 16G, 32I 2 strips 1½ by 46½ inches, 2 strips 1½ by 48½ inches (seams included)
6. off-white with brown dot	1¾ yards	20D, 32E, 32J, 4K, 4Kr, 28L, 4M Binding strips: leave 7 by 60 inches uncut
7. Backing	3¼ yards	

"r" indicates the reverse side of a pattern piece
¼-inch seam allowances are not included unless indicated.

FINISHED SIZE: 54 BY 54 INCHES

PIECING INSTRUCTIONS

1. Using the Pattern Pieces provided, trace and cut pieces according to the Cutting Instructions. Add ¼ inch for seam allowances before cutting. Follow the Color Placement Guide and the Quilt Block drawing to assemble.

2. Sew two C pieces onto an A (figure 4-124).

3. In the corners of each of the nine blocks is a D piece or the equivalent EEFG. Consult the Guide when making each block to see how many of each you will need.

Set a D or EEFG into the open V-shaped end of a B piece. To do this, pin and then sew from the right to the center, pivot and then pin and sew from the center to the left side (figure 4-125).

4. Join two of each of these units as shown in figure 4-126. This is half a block.

5. Repeat Steps 2 through 4. Join together along the Q seam.

6. Repeat Steps 2 through 5 for each of the nine blocks, using the D or EEFG as indicated in the Guide.

7. Sew the nine blocks together using the Guide.

Border 1: ½-inch border

Sew the two 1- by 45½-inch dark print strips down the two sides of the quilt. Then add the two 1- by 46½-inch strips across the top and bottom.

Border 2: 1-inch border

Sew the two 1½- by 46½-inch peach strips down the sides. Then add the two 1½- by 48½-inch strips across the top and bottom.

4-124. Piecing together two Cs and A.

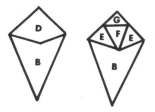

4-125. Piecing together D and B, or EEFG and B.

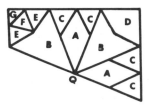

4-126. Join two of these units to two CACs.

4-127. Color Placement Guide.

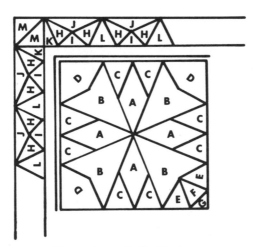

4-128. Fifteen-inch Quilt Block.

Border 3: pieced border

1. Join an H to an I as shown in figure 4-130.

2. Join a J to an H as shown in figure 4-130.

3. Set the H/I into the J/H (figure 4-131). See page 21 for directions on how to *set in*.

4. Sew the L to the H (figure 4-131).

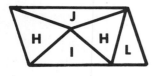

4-129. The pieces for the border.
4-130. Piecing together H and I; piecing together J and H.
4-131. Piecing together HI, HJ, and L.

5. Repeat Steps 1 through 4 seven more times to make one border strip, beginning and ending each strip with a K or Kr (figure 4-132).

6. Make four of these strips. Sew two of them down the sides of the quilt (figure 4-133). Add the squares shown in the drawing to each end of the other two border strips using the Color Placement Guide. Sew these two strips across the top and bottom of the quilt.

4-132. Piecing together the border strip.

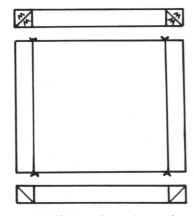

4-133. Placing the strip on the quilt.

QUILTING

With a hard pencil (#2 or #3) mark lines ¼ inch from the seams in all of the Pattern Pieces except for the Bs. When two of the D pieces come together, they form a large light area. Use the quilting pattern indicated by dotted lines on the D pattern piece to quilt these areas.

Layer and baste using the directions given in Chapter 1. Quilt.

FINISHING

To bind this quilt, use the polka dot fabric and follow the directions for a separate binding (see page 27).

VARIATION

This design can easily be enlarged for any size bed quilt by adding more of the 15-inch blocks. When you do add blocks, be sure to change the D pieces to EEFG pieces whenever a complete octagon is formed. Adjust the borders to the increased number of blocks.

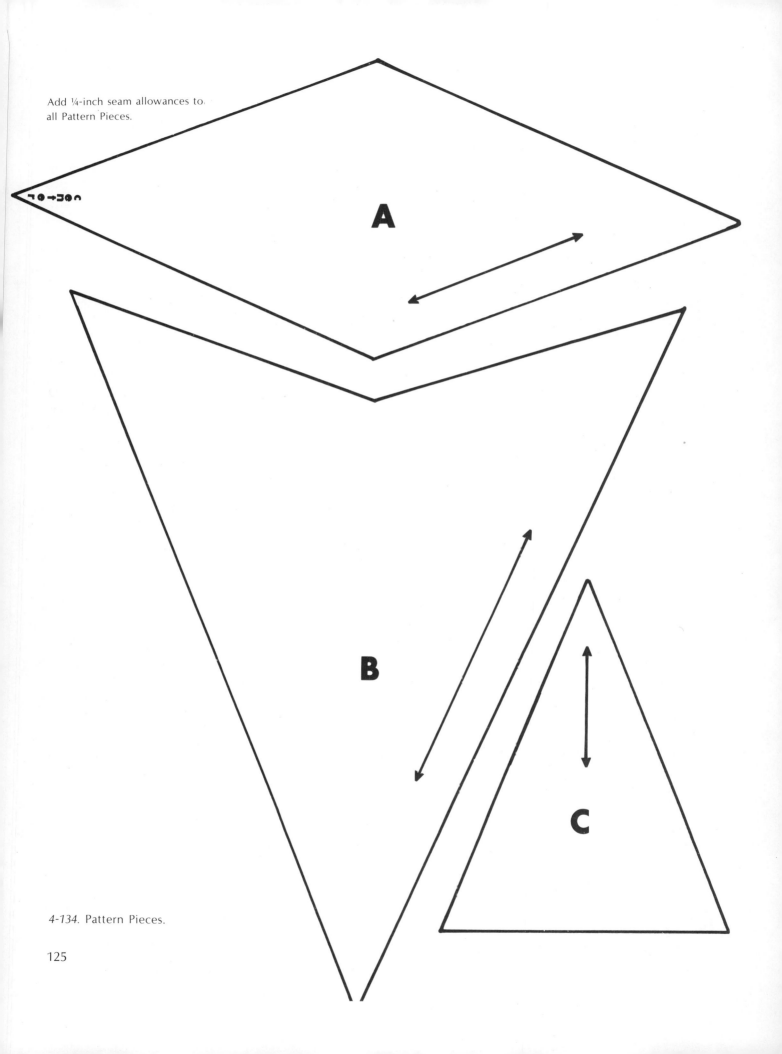

Add ¼-inch seam allowances to all Pattern Pieces.

Straight of Goods

A

B

C

4-134. Pattern Pieces.

125

Add ¼-inch seam allowances to all Pattern Pieces.

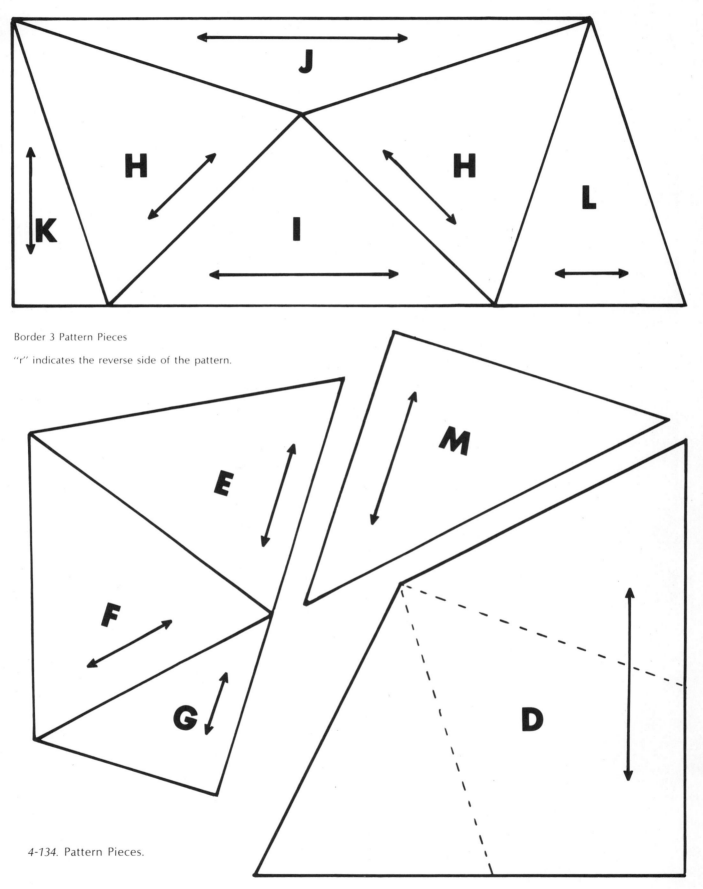

Border 3 Pattern Pieces

"r" indicates the reverse side of the pattern.

4-134. Pattern Pieces.

Dotted lines on Pattern Piece D indicates quilting pattern.

AMETHYSTINE

The evolution of this design is described in the chapter on design. After you have pieced the 12½-inch blocks, try rotating them to create different arrangements before you sew them together. Besides the full-size pattern pieces, a draft of the design is included to enable you to increase or decrease the size of the blocks.

4-135. **Amethystine.** Designed by Sheila Meyer.

MATERIALS AND CUTTING CHART

Fabrics	Yardage	Cutting Instructions
1. ivory	1¼ yards	16A, 16Ar, 16D, 16Dr, 16F, 16Fr
2. pink	1⅓ yards	16C, 16Cr
3. purple	1½ yards	16G, 16Gr
		Binding strips: leave 6 inches by
		54 inches uncut
4. navy	1 yard	16B, 16Br, 16E, 16Er
5. Backing	3 yards	

"r" indicates the reverse side of the pattern.
¼-inch seam allowances are not included.

FINISHED SIZE: 50 BY 50 INCHES

4-136. Color Placement Guide.

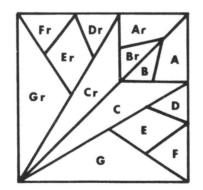

4-137. The 12½-inch Quilt Block.

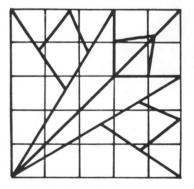

4-138. Draft of design.

PIECING INSTRUCTIONS

1. Using the Pattern Pieces provided, trace and cut pieces according to the Cutting Instructions (figure 4-137 and 4-138). Add ¼-inch seam allowances before cutting.

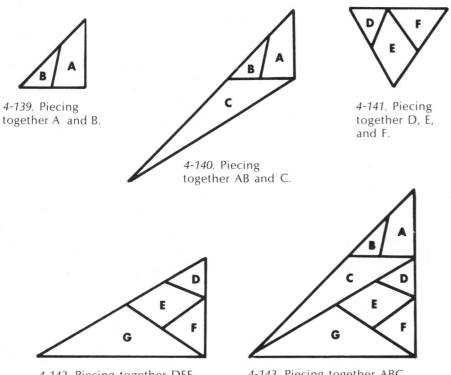

4-139. Piecing
together A and B.

4-140. Piecing
together AB and C.

4-141. Piecing
together D, E,
and F.

4-142. Piecing together DEF
and G.

4-143. Piecing together ABC
and DEFG.

2. Join an ivory A to a navy B (figure 4-139).

3. Sew the AB to a pink C (figure 4-140).

4. Sew an ivory D and an ivory F onto a navy E as shown in figure 4-141.

5. Sew this DEF piece to a purple G (figure 4-142).

6. Bring these two units together and sew (figure 4-143). This completes half a block.

7. Repeat Steps 1 through 6 using the reversed side of the pattern pieces marked "r."

8. Sew these two halves together down the center diagonal line.

9. Repeat Steps 1 through 8 to form each of the sixteen identical blocks.

10. Assemble the blocks according to the Color Placement Guide.

QUILTING

Suggested quilting patterns are indicated by dotted lines on the Pattern Pieces. Transfer markings onto the quilt.

Layer and baste the quilt, referring to Chapter 1 for information on layering. Quilt as marked.

FINISHING

Bind this quilt using the purple fabric and follow the directions given for separate bindings (see page 27).

Add ¼-inch seam allowances to all Pattern Pieces.

"r" indicates the reverse side of the pattern.

Dotted lines inside indicate quilting pattern.

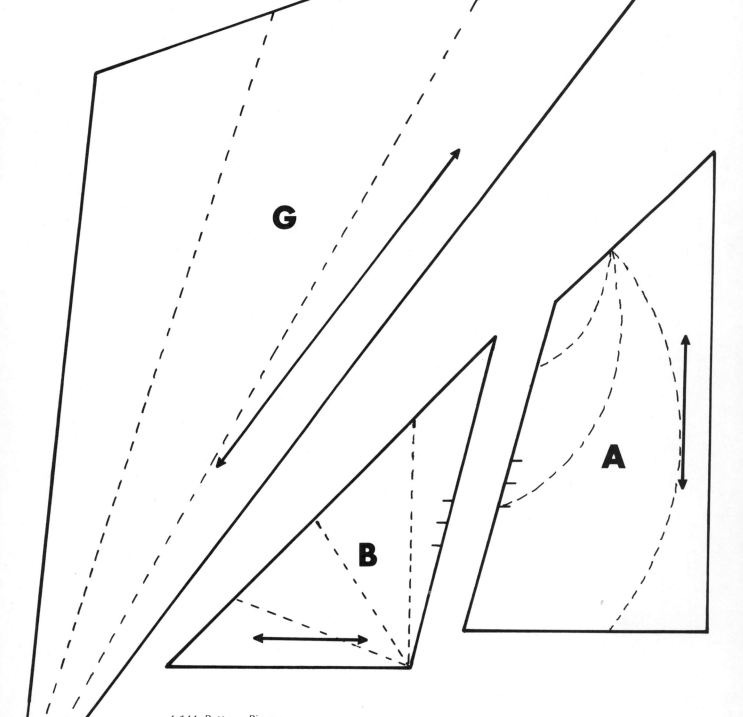

4-144. Pattern Pieces.

When complete, Pattern Piece C should look like this.

"r" indicates the reverse side of the pattern.

C

Tape pieces together at dotted line xy to form Pattern Piece C.

Add ¼-inch seam allowance at solid lines.

4-144. Pattern Pieces.

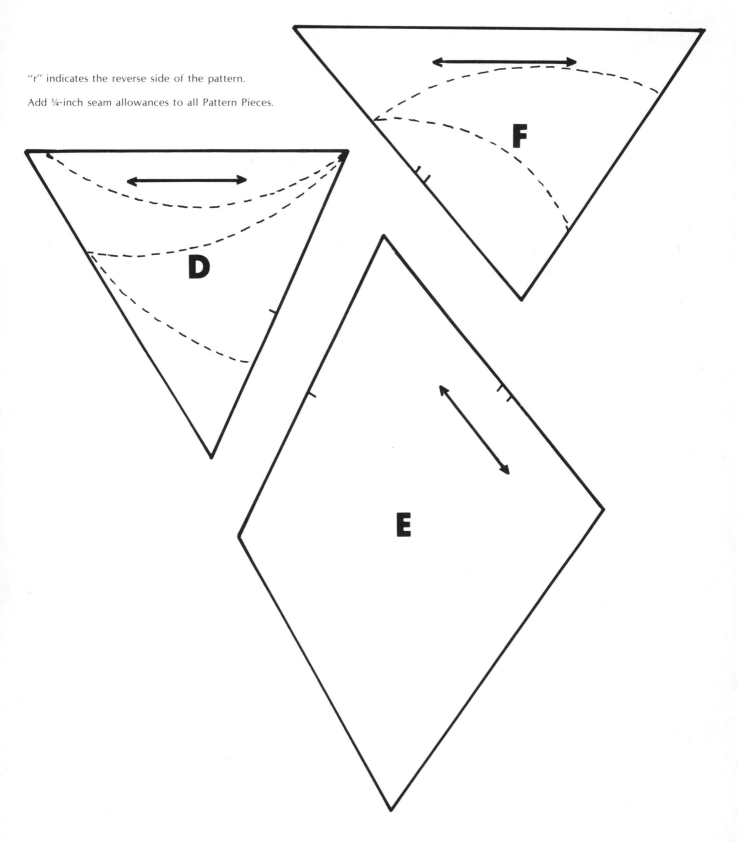

"r" indicates the reverse side of the pattern.

Add ¼-inch seam allowances to all Pattern Pieces.

D

F

E

4-144. Pattern Pieces.

IN THE PINK

In the Pink is a monochromatic exercise. The quilt incorporates shades of red from burgundy to lavender to orange into a harmonious union. The design itself is reminiscent of a city skyline, the hues suggesting a city at dawn or a rosy dusk.

4-145. **In the Pink.** Designed by Judy Robbins.

Since **In the Pink** has very simple geometric shapes, it is not necessary to make templates. Calculate the dimensions of each piece by looking at the graphed drawing (figure 4-150). Each square equals one inch. For example, the pale pink rectangle in the upper left corner is 6 squares by 12 squares, or 6 inches by 12 inches. Using a ruler (a see-through plastic T-shaped ruler is especially helpful) and a soft pencil, mark the 6-inch by 12-inch rectangle on the straight grain of the wrong side of the pink fabric. Cut ¼ inch beyond this pencil line all around to allow for seams. The pencil line will be your sewing line. Consulting the Color Placement Guide (figure 4-149), and the graphed drawing (figure 4-150), calculate, mark, and cut all the pieces. From burgundy fabric, cut two borders 3 inches by 34½ inches. Cut two more borders 44½ inches by 3 inches. These border measurements include seam allowances.

FINISHED SIZE: 40 BY 44 INCHES

MATERIALS CHART

Fabrics	Yardage
1. pale pink	¼ yard
2. pale peach	¼ yard
3. medium peach	¼ yard
4. hot pink	¼ yard
5. lavender	⅛ yard
6. light mauve	¼ yard
7. dark mauve	¼ yard
8. medium rust	½ yard
9. dusty rose	¼ yard
10. burgundy	¾ yard
11. Backing	1 yard

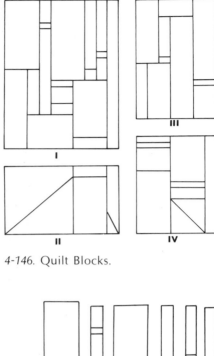

4-146. Quilt Blocks.

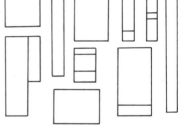

4-147. Piecing together Section I (step 1).

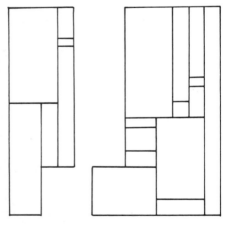

4-148. Piecing together Section I (step 2).

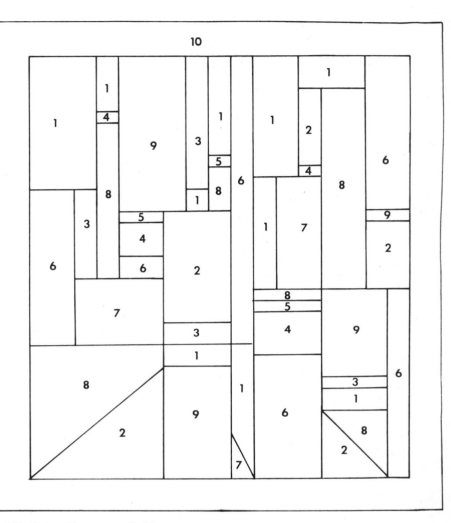

4-149. Color Placement Guide.

PIECING INSTRUCTIONS

1. This quilt is pieced in four sections (figure 4-146). Each section is divided into smaller units. Following the Color Placement Guide, lay out Section I on your sewing table. Keeping ¼-inch seams (that is, sewing on the pencil lines) piece the smaller units as shown in figure 4-147.

2. Sew these small units together to make two larger units (figure 4-148).

3. Sew these two units together. This seam has two set-in corners, places where the needle must pivot to make a square corner (see arrows figure 4-151). This seam will be manageable if you sew it in three steps. First (1) pin the short vertical seam at the bottom, and sew. Then (2) pin and sew the short horizontal seam. Finally (3) pin and sew the long remaining vertical seam. Some people find it easiest to sew seams with pivot points by hand.

1. Lay out and sew Section II as shown in figure 4-152.

5. Lay out and sew Section III as shown in figure 4-153.

6. Lay out and sew Section IV as shown in figure 4-154.

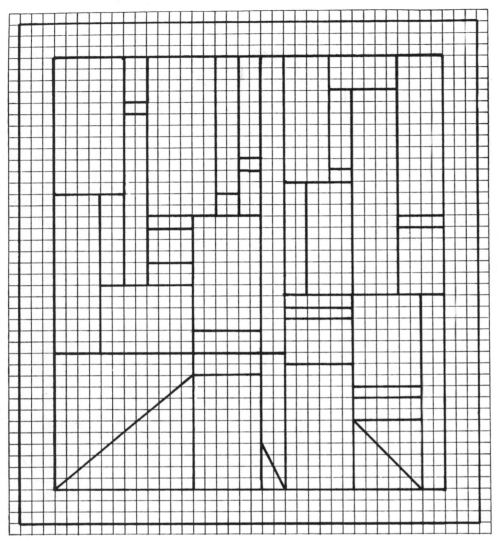

4-150. Graphed Drawing. Each square equals 1 inch.

7. Sew the four sections together.

8. Pin and sew burgundy borders all around.

9. Press pieced top carefully. While you press, trim away any stray threads from the back.

QUILTING

The triangles and rectangles of **In the Pink** are quilted with straight lines spaced evenly apart within the individual shapes. Mark the quilting lines on the pieced top with a ruler and a hard pencil.

Layer the backing, batting, and top. Baste and quilt.

FINISHING

Apply a separate binding (see page 27). Use burgundy strips to match the border.

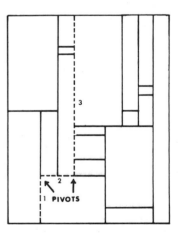

4-151. Piecing together Section I (step 3).

135

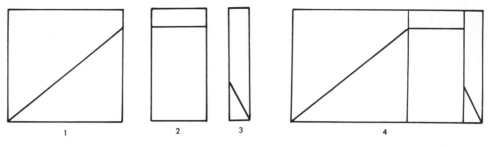

4-152. Piecing together Section II.

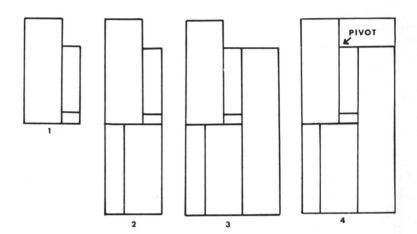

4-153. Piecing together Section III.

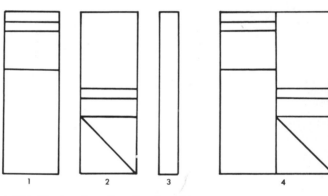

4-154. Piecing together Section IV.

VARIATIONS

Of course **In the Pink** needn't always be pink. Any other monochromatic color scheme would look equally attractive, but combinations of different colors can change the look entirely. Whatever colors you choose, the idea presented in this project—sewing simple geometric shapes together—is the essence of patchwork. This could be a wonderful scrapbag project, the shapes planned on graph paper to cover an area about 60 inches by 72 inches. This size makes a generous lap quilt for folding over a sofa in the den or playroom.

136

OPTRIC

The drama of this small wall hanging depends on precision piecing and intense colors. **Optric** is heavily quilted with curving designs (indicated on the Pattern Pieces) which soften the sharp angles and create another area of interest.

4-155. **Optric.** Designed by Judy Robbins.

MATERIALS AND CUTTING CHART

Fabrics	Yardage	Cutting Instructions
1. magenta	½ yard	28B
2. peach	½ yard	1A, 12D
3. navy	1 yard	4C, 8E, 4F
4. Backing	1 yard	

Letters indicate pattern pieces. Numbers indicate colors.
¼-inch seam allowances are not included.

FINISHED SIZE: 36 BY 36 INCHES

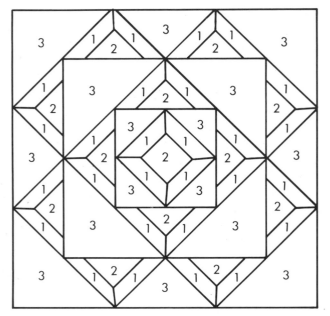

4-156. Color Placement Guide.

4-157. Block Placement Guide.

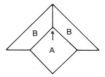

4-158. Piecing together two Bs and A.

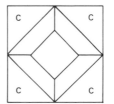

4-159. Adding four Cs to the BA block.

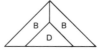

4-160. Piecing together two Bs and D.

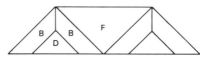

4-161. Piecing together two BD blocks and F.

PIECING INSTRUCTIONS

1. Using the Pattern Pieces provided, trace and cut pieces according to Cutting Instructions. Add ¼-inch seam allowances before cutting.

2. Seam two Bs to center square A. Then sew the small seam to join B to B (see arrow, figure 4-158). This seam is tricky to sew by machine. Even if you machine piece the rest of the wall hanging, you may want to sew the BB seams by hand.

3. Sew two more Bs to A. Join BB seams.

4. Sew four C triangles to existing unit (figure 4-159).

5. Sew two Bs to a D triangle, and join the BB seam (figure 4-160). Make three others like this one.

6. Sew these BD triangles to the ABC base unit.

7. Sew four large E triangles to the base unit.

8. Repeat Step 5.

9. Join two BD units to an F triangle (figure 4-161). Sew this to the base unit. Repeat three times.

10. Sew four E triangles to the base unit.

QUILTING

Press carefully. Trim any stray threads from the back of the pieced area. Mark the quilting design, following the dotted lines on the Pattern Pieces.

Layer the backing, batting, and top. Baste. Quilt, following the marked design.

FINISHING

Bind the edges in navy fabric. Use separate binding technique (page 27). A casing is recommended for hanging the finished piece (see page 35).

Quilting pattern for Pattern Piece E.

To make Pattern Piece E, draw a 12-inch square and cut it in half diagonally. Then add seam allowance.

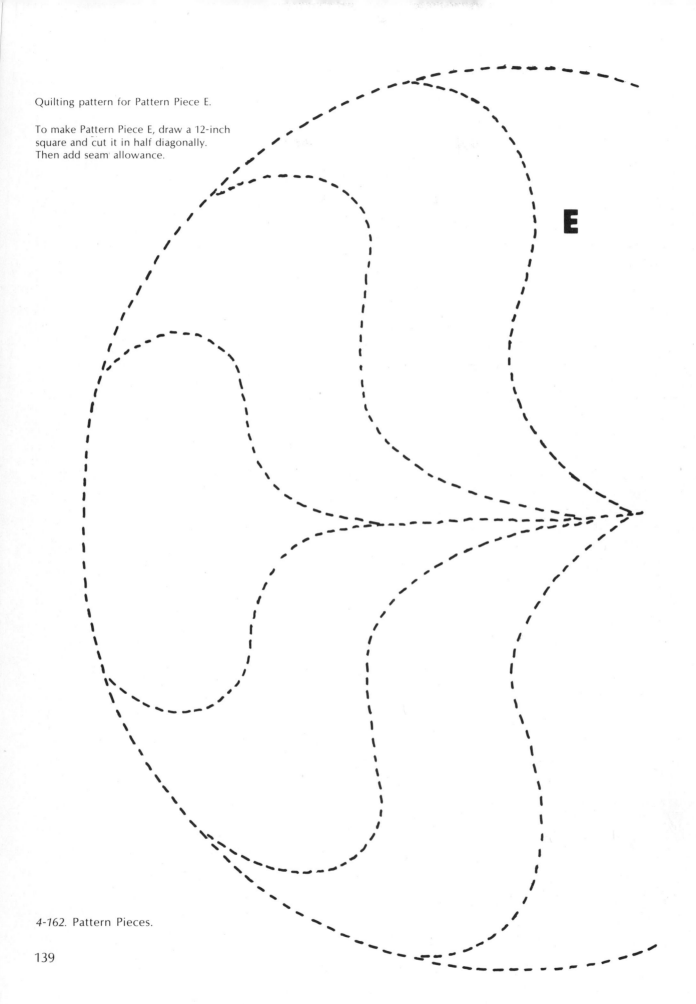

E

4-162. Pattern Pieces.

Add ¼-inch seam allowances to all Pattern Pieces.

Dotted lines indicate quilting pattern.

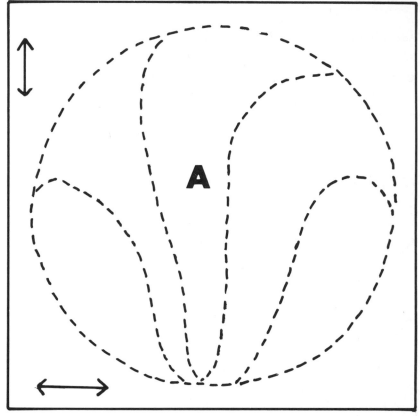

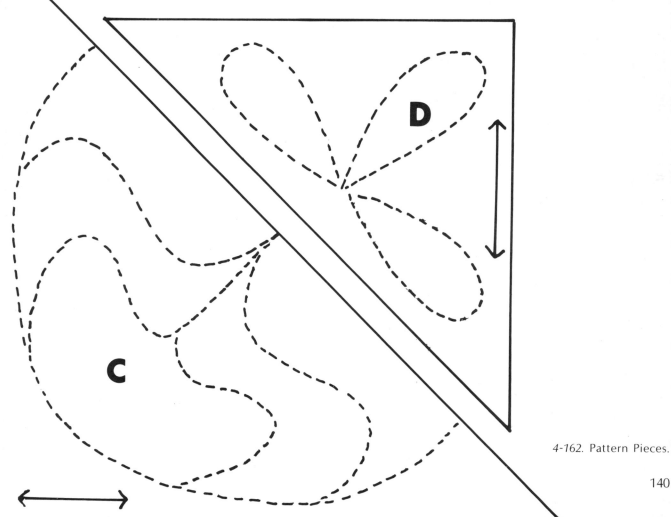

4-162. Pattern Pieces.

Add ¼-inch seam allowances to all Pattern Pieces.

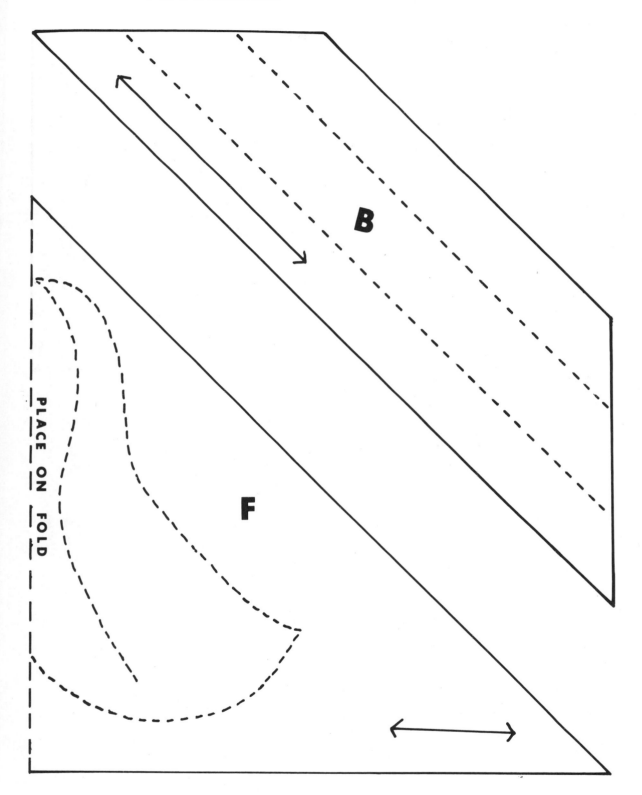

PEACE DANCE

This design has a Native American theme. The quilt is made of two different blocks—a 12-inch central medallion, surrounded by 6-inch border blocks. The smaller blocks are rotated, creating a motion around the edges which suggests rhythmic dancing.

4-163. **Peace Dance.** Designed by Judy Robbins.

MATERIALS AND CUTTING CHART

Fabric	Yardage	Cutting Instructions
1. dark red	½ yard	4A, 12F, 36H
2. light blue	½ yard	4B, 8H
3. medium blue	½ yard	4C, 4F, 20H
4. indigo	1 yard	4D, 4E, 8F, 12G, 8H
		Borders: 2 strips 2½ by 24½ inches, 2 strips 2½ by 26 ½ inches (seams included)
5. Backing	1 yard	

Letters indicate Pattern Pieces. Numbers indicate colors.
¼ inch seam allowances are not included unless indicated.

FINISHED SIZE: 28 BY 28 INCHES

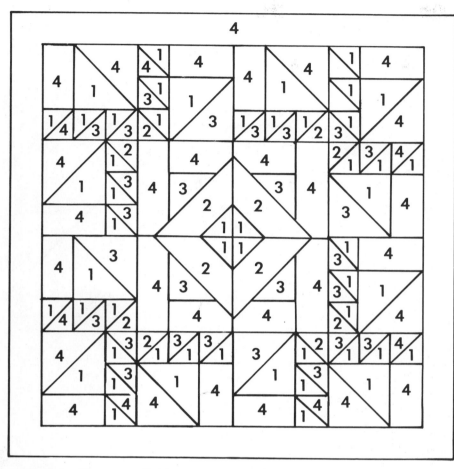

4-164. Color Placement Guide.

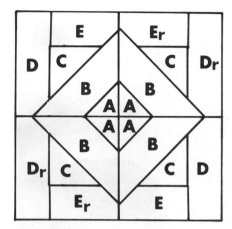

4-165. Twelve-inch Quilt Block.

4-166. Six-inch Border Quilt Block.

PIECING INSTRUCTIONS

1. Using the Pattern Pieces provided, trace and cut pieces according to Cutting Instructions. Add ¼-inch seam allowances before cutting. Make 12-inch center block as follows: seam A to short side of B (figure 4-167). Repeat three times.

2. Seam C to E (figure 4-168). Repeat three times.

3. Seam D to CE (figure 4-169). Repeat three times.

4. Seam AB to CDE (figure 4-170). Repeat three times.

5. Carefully matching seams, join one ABCDE unit to another (figure 4-171). Repeat. Sew these two-block units together to form the central medallion (see Quilt Block).

6. Following the Color Placement Guide (figure 4-164), lay out each 6-inch block on your sewing table. Piece as follows.

7. Sew two Fs together. Add a G (figure 4-172).

8. Sew two Hs together. Repeat two times.

9. Sew HH unit to FFG unit to form a 6-inch block. Repeat for all 6-inch blocks.

10. Following the Guide, lay out all the 6-inch blocks around the 12-inch

4-167. Piecing together A and B.

4-168. Piecing together C and E.

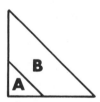

4-169. Piecing together D and CE.

4-170. Piecing together AB and DCE.

143

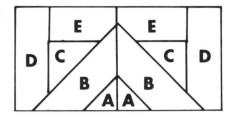

4-171. Piecing together two units.

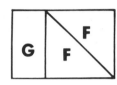

4-172. Piecing together two Fs and G.

center block. Keeping the blocks in order, seam two together. Sew to the side of the 12-inch block. Repeat. The unit will look like figure 4-173.

11. Sew four 6-inch blocks together. Matching seams, sew to the top of the existing unit. Repeat with remaining four blocks for the bottom row.

12. Sew borders to sides. Press.

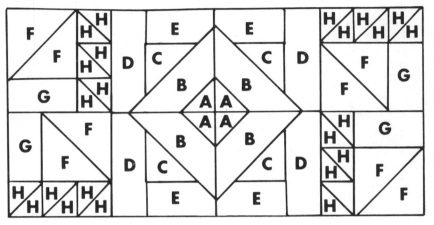

4-173. The finished center.

QUILTING

Mark the quilting design on the center block. One fourth of the quilting design is shown in dotted lines on the Pattern Pieces. Repeat this design in the quadrants of the center block.

The remainder of the indigo area is quilted with straight lines 1 inch apart. The medium blue trangles are quilted with lines ½ inch apart. Mark these lines, if desired.

Layer the backing, batting, and top. Baste. Quilt, following the marked lines.

FINISHING

Bind the edges of the quilt with a separate straight binding (see page 27).

VARIATIONS

The central block of this wall hanging makes a handsome quilt when used alone. Set solid, the blocks create the appearance of indigo lattice strips. The light blue square seems to have been laid on top of the indigo "lattice," creating a three-dimensional effect.

Another possibility would be to make a bed quilt by enlarging the scale of the wall hanging, making the medallion 18 inches and the smaller blocks 9 inches. Other rows of border blocks can be added as necessary to fit your bed. Traditional sawtooth borders (figure 4-174) also complement this versatile design.

4-174. Traditional sawtooth border.

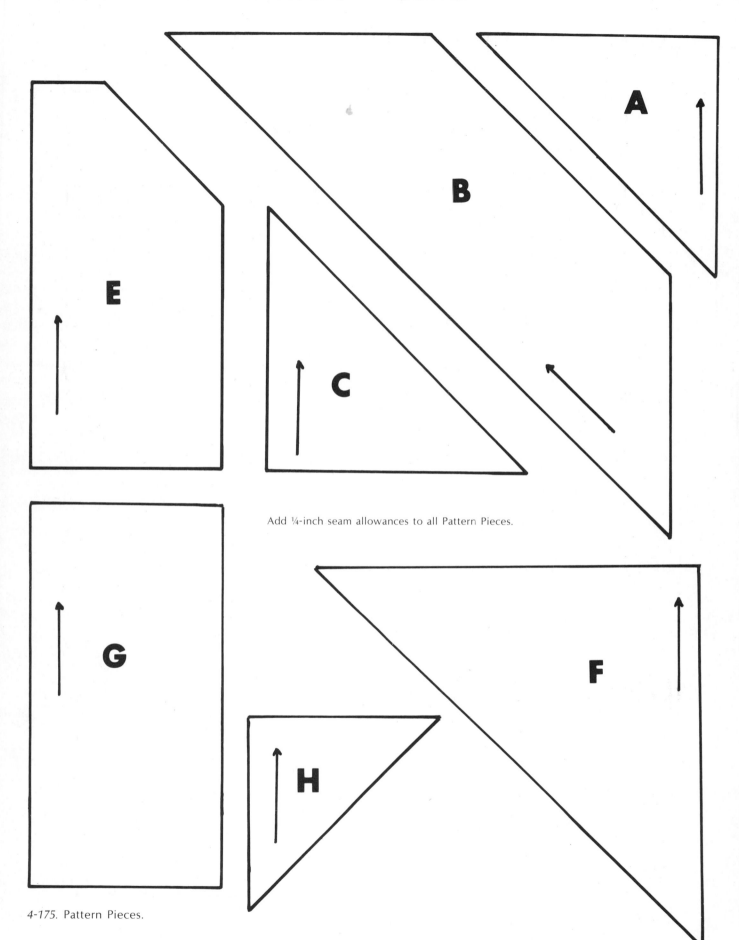

Add ¼-inch seam allowances to all Pattern Pieces.

4-175. Pattern Pieces.

Add ¼-inch seam allowances to all Pattern Pieces.

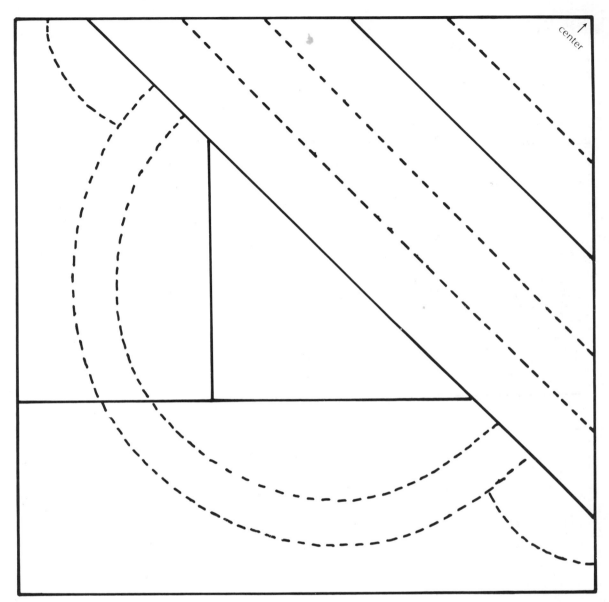

Dotted lines indicate quilting pattern. One-quarter of center block is shown. Transfer quilting lines to center block.

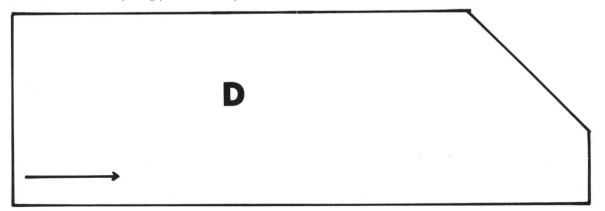

4-175. Pattern Pieces.

RIVER RUN

River Run translates into fabric the tumbling of a stream over falls. The appealing asymmetrical design is made in shades of blue and green against a white background.

4-176. **River Run.** Designed by Judy Robbins.

MATERIALS AND CUTTING CHART

Fabrics	Yardage	Cutting Instructions
1. white	1½ yards	1Ab, 1B, 7C, 1D, 1E Borders: 2 strips 3 by 51½ inches, 2 strips 3 by 56½ inches (seams included)
2. turquoise	¾ yard	2A, 8B, 12C, 2F
3. sea green	¾ yard	1A, 4B, 6C, 1F
4. ocean blue	¾ yard	1A, 4B, 6C, 1F Borders: 2 strips 1½ by 49½ inches, 2 strips 1½ by 51½ inches (seams included)
5. Backing (use white, as above)	3¼ yards	

Letters indicate Pattern Pieces. Numbers indicate colors.
¼-inch seam allowances are not included unless indicated.

FINISHED SIZE: 56 BY 56 INCHES

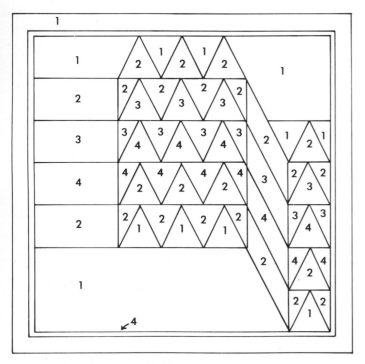

4-177. Color Placement Guide.

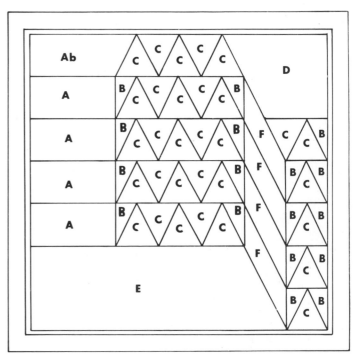

4-178. Block Placement Guide.

PIECING INSTRUCTIONS

This quilt is made in sections, as shown in the Piecing Together Diagrams.

1. Using the Pattern Pieces provided, trace and cut pieces according to Cutting Instructions. Add ¼-inch seam allowances before cutting. Following the Color Placement Guide, lay out the large BC area (Section I) near your sewing table. It is made of B and C triangles sewn together in five rows. Row by row, seam these triangles together until your finished unit looks like Section I (figure 4-178).

2. Following the Guide, lay out and seam A blocks (Section II), adding the Ab block to the top.

3. Make Section III by laying out the B and C triangles according to the Color Guide. Sew.

4. Section IV consists of F pieces. These are long and thin and may stretch, so be sure to sew the seams carefully, without pulling or stretching at all.

5. To make Section V, sew the lower portion (CCB). Then join to D.

6. Begin joining the sections by sewing Section I to II. Pin carefully, matching seams. There is one pivot point where Ab meets a row of Cs. Many people find this tricky to do on the machine. You may choose to sew this portion of the seam by hand.

7. Pin section IV to section I, matching seams. Sew.

8. Join section III to section IV, matching seams.

9. Sew section V to existing unit. There will be one pivot point in this seam.

10. Then sew the large E piece to the existing unit (one pivot point).

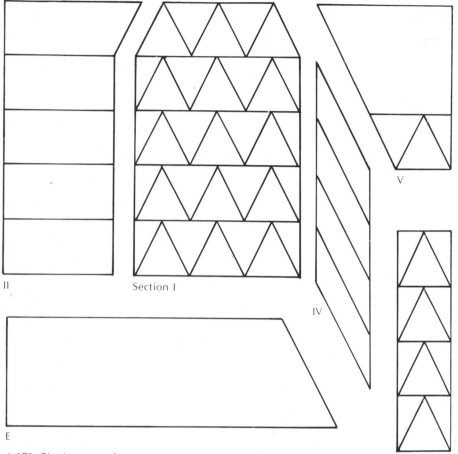

II   Section I   IV   V   III

4-179. Piecing together.

11. Sew the blue border all around.
12. Finally sew the white border all around.

QUILTING AND FINISHING

Press carefully, and trim any stray threads from the seamed side.

To make the backing, cut the 3¼ yards of white backing fabric in half to make two 60-inch lengths. Seam these together to make a piece 60 by approximately 89 inches. This seam will be centered on the back of the quilt.

Layer the backing, batting, and the pieced top. Trim the extra backing fabric away from each side. Baste.

Outline quilt, following the zigzag lines of the design. You may want to quilt the white area with lines about 3 inches apart, echoing the zigzags. Bind with a separate straight binding (see page 27).

VARIATIONS

This quilt is 56 inches square. Made in rainbow hues or birght primary colors, it would be a suitable nap quilt for a young child. The size can be extended by adding borders to make a twin-bed quilt.

Add ¼-inch seam allowances to all Pattern Pieces.

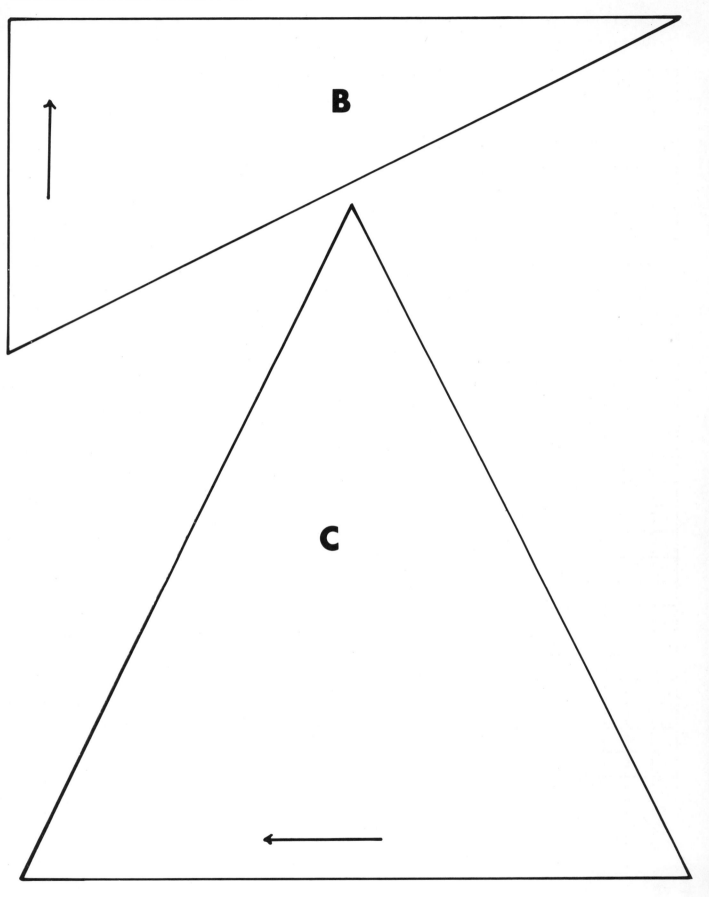

4-180. Pattern Pieces.

Pattern Pieces A, Ab, F, D, and E are *not* full size.

Enlarge them by letting each square equal 1 ¾ inches.

Then add ¼-inch seam allowances.

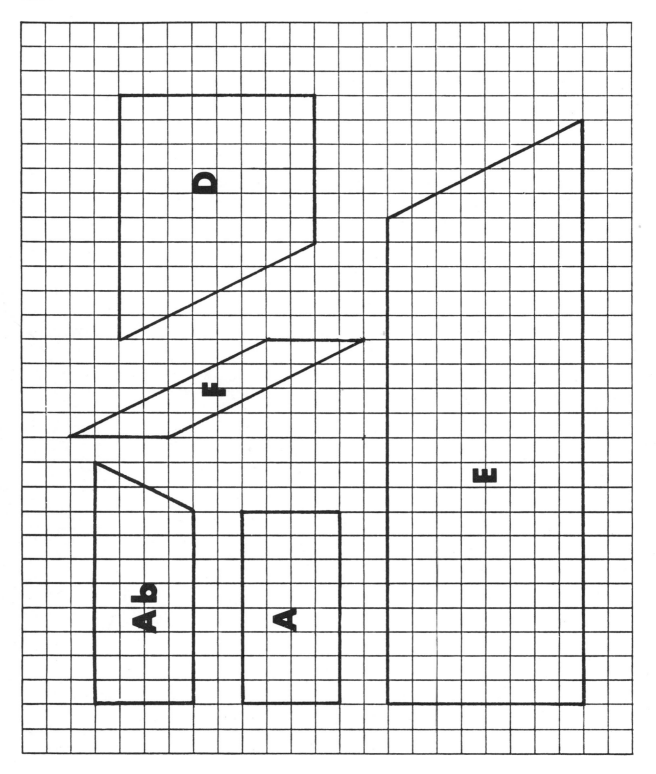

SUNLIGHT THROUGH THE TREES

In this design, yellow sunlight shines on the top of the quilt and filters through the green of the "trees." The thickening leaves admit less light at the bottom of the piece, so it is light on the top and dark at the bottom. Keeping this in mind, freely substitute fabrics you may have on hand.

4-181. **Sunlight Through the Trees.** Designed by Judy Robbins.

MATERIALS AND CUTTING CHART

Fabrics	Yardage	Cutting Instructions
1. light yellow	¼ yard	4B, 2C
2. medium yellow	¼ yard	1A, 8B, 6C
3. yellow gingham	¼ yard	12B, 2C
4. yellow calico	¼ yard	9B, 3C
5. green calico	¼ yard	6B, 4C
6. yellow-green	¼ yard	2A, 6B, 5C
7. dark green	¼ yard	6B, 5C
8. grass green	¾ yard	1A, 13B, 3C
9. Backing	1 yard	*Borders: 2 strips 3½ by 30½ inches, 2 strips 3½ by 24½ inches (seams included)

¼-inch seam allowances are not included unless indicated.
*Add an extra inch in length to these borders when cutting to allow for piecing discrepancies. This can be trimmed off after the borders are pinned in place.

FINISHED SIZE: 30 BY 30 INCHES

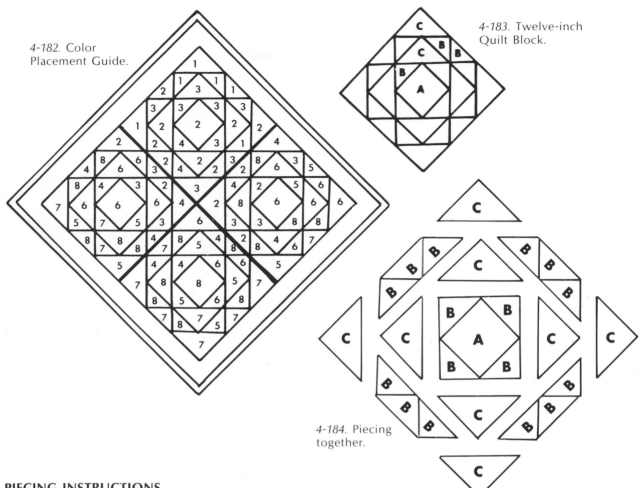

4-182. Color Placement Guide.

4-183. Twelve-inch Quilt Block.

4-184. Piecing together.

PIECING INSTRUCTIONS

1. Using the Pattern Pieces provided, trace and cut pieces according to Cutting Instructions. Add ¼-inch seam allowances before cutting.

2. This design is easy to piece if it is kept in blocks (see Quilt Block). The heavy lines in the Color Placement Guide show where each block ends. Following the Guide, lay out the pieces for each block puzzle-fashion, on your sewing table. Sew one block at a time.

3. Sew four Bs to an A.

4. Sew four Cs to the AB unit.

5. Sew three Bs together. Then sew this three-B unit to the ABC unit. Repeat around the ABC unit, sewing a three-B unit to each side.

6. Finish the block by sewing Cs into the corners to form a square.

7. Construct four of these blocks and sew them together to form the design shown in the Color Placement Guide.

8. Sew grass green borders all around.

FINISHING

Layer the backing, batting, and the pieced top. Baste. Outline quilt and remove basting. Bind the edges, using a separate binding (see page 27).

153

VARIATION

A beautiful quilt can be made by making four of these four-block units and sewing them together with all of the pale yellows in the center. The sunlight, then, appears to be shining through the center of the quilt, radiating toward the edges. Several borders should be added to make the quilt bed-size.

Add ¼-inch seam allowances to all Pattern Pieces.

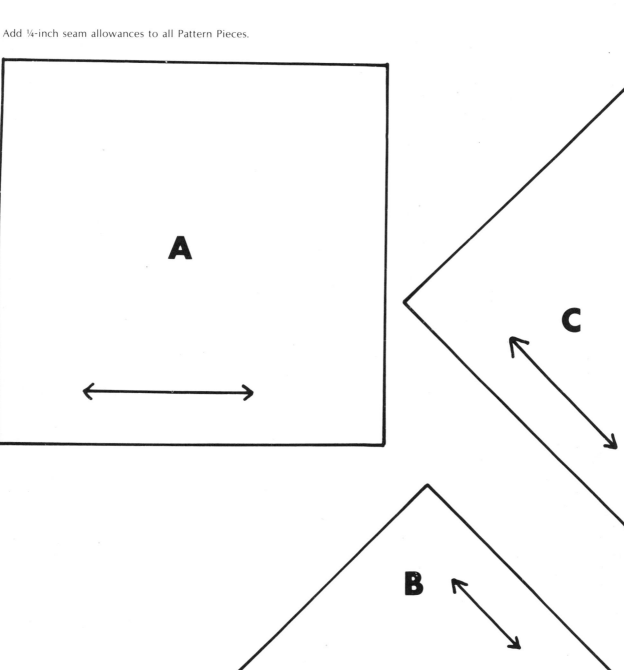

4-185. Pattern Pieces.

Glossary

Armature: A wooden support of ¼-inch plywood that is cut to the contours of the upper portion of an oddly shaped quilt and extends to its widest part.

Backing: The bottom of the three layers of a quilt, visible as the back of the quilt, usually one large sheet of fabric to accommodate size or shaping.

Banner Method: A method for hanging quilts using fabric loops and dowels or curtain rods.

Baste (verb): To temporarily stitch fabric together before permanent stitching is complete.

Batting (or **Batt**): A cotton or polyester filler used as the middle layer in a quilt to add body and warmth.

Binding: Encasing the raw edges of a quilt by attaching long strips of fabric.

Bias: Fabric grain runs lengthwise and crosswise. The true bias runs diagonally to these lines.

Blind Stitch: Nearly invisible stitch used frequently for appliqué or hemming.

Block: A section of a quilt usually made from several geometric shapes that forms one complete design.

Border: Plain or pieced strips attached to all sides of a quilt that act as a frame for the design.

Butting: Attaching binding so that the corners are squared off, not mitered. Also, feeding pairs of pieces under the presser foot of the sewing machine without lifting the presser foot or clipping connecting threads.

Casing: See **Sleeve**.

Contour Casing: Casings that are shaped to the contours of the quilt.

Dowel: A long, unfinished round length of wood which is available in many diameters.

Draft: To draw, plan, or sketch a design of something to be made.

Duct Tape: Wide, sturdy aluminum tape used for fastening the back of a quilt to foamcore board.

Even-feed Foot: A sewing-machine attachment that allows top and bottom fabric to feed through the machine at the same rate.

Firring Strip: Narrow strip of thin wood that can be cut to length and used in a sleeve to hang a quilt. Also called Lattice Strips.

Foam Board: A lightweight styrene foam sheet 3/16-inch thick covered on both sides with heavy white paper.

Grain Line: The lengthwise grain of fabric as it comes off the bolt. Crosswise grain runs perpendicular to this line.

Hand Quilting: Small running stitches done by hand that hold the three layers of a quilt together. Their purpose is both functional and decorative.

Hard Mounting: Any of several methods used to mount quilts when a firm or rigid look is desired, such as purchased frames, stretchers, or armatures.

Lattice: See **Firring Strip**.

Masonite: Thin, hard fiber board sometimes used for mounting irregularly shaped quilts.

Miter: Joining of two pieces of fabric at the corners by folding or seaming, usually at a 45-degree angle. Often refers to borders or binding.

Piece (verb): To join geometric pieces of fabric together as part of the process of making a quilt.

Plexiglass: Clear, hard plastic that comes in sheet form and may be cut into shapes with a saw.

Quilt (verb): To join the three layers (top, batting, and backing) of a quilt together with either hand or machine stitches.

Sashing: Fabric strips sewn between quilt blocks. These strips frame and separate each block.

Selvage: The narrow, tightly woven edge of the fabric as it comes from the bolt.

Set-in: A method of joining pieces that contain angles that do not permit sewing a continuous straight seam.

Sleeve: A separate piece of fabric sewn to the back of a quilt through which a firring strip or curtain rod can be inserted to facilitate hanging.

Soft-mounting: Any of several methods used to support a quilt for hanging without losing the soft appearance of the quilt, as in casing, sleeve, or banner methods.

Stabbing: A method of hand quilting whereby the needle is inserted from top to bottom, then reinserted from bottom to top to complete a single stitch.

Stay-stitching: Machine stitching on raw edges of fabric near the seam line to prevent stretching or fraying, especially helpful to stabilize bias edges.

Stitch-in-the-ditch: Top-stitching done over an existing seam line so that it is barely visible.

Stretchers: Wooden slats that are shaped and grooved for mounting fabric or canvas.

Template: A pattern made of cardboard, plastic, metal, or other firm material cut accurately in the shape of a geometric piece of a quilt to provide consistently identical shapes.

Truing-up: Aligning a quilt which has been distorted because of overpressing, bias stretch, or uneven seam allowances.

Tying: Fastening the three layers of a quilt together at regular intervals by tying with small pieces of yarn or string. A faster, easier method for holding a quilt together than quilting, but far less durable. Sometimes referred to as Tufting.

Velcro: A nylon fastener consisting of two self-adhering strips.

Metric Conversion Chart

	True Metric	Approximate Metric
¼ inch	6.35mm	6mm
⅜ inch	9.5mm	1cm
1 inch	2.54cm	2.5cm
2 inch	5.08cm	5cm
3 inch	7.62cm	7.5cm
4 inch	10.16cm	10cm
5 inch	12.70cm	12.5cm
6 inch	15.24cm	15.25cm
7 inch	17.78cm	17.75cm
8 inch	20.32cm	20.5cm
9 inch	22.86cm	22.75cm
10 inch	25.4cm	25.5cm
12 inch	30.48cm	30.5cm

Index